SPORTS WRITER'S EYE

MATTHEW ENGEL

SPORTS WRITER'S EYE

AN ANTHOLOGY

Macdonald
Queen Anne Press

A *Queen Anne Press* Book

© Matthew Engel 1989

First published in Great Britain in 1989 by
Queen Anne Press, a division of
Macdonald & Co (Publishers) Ltd
66-73 Shoe Lane
London EC4P 4AB

A member of Maxwell Pergamon Publishing Corporation plc

British Library Cataloguing in Publication Data
Engel, Matthew
   Sportswriter's eye : an anthology.
   1. Sports
   I. Title
   796

ISBN 0–356–17844–7

Photoset in North Wales by
Derek Doyle & Associates, Mold, Clwyd
Printed and bound in Great Britain by
BPCC Hazell Books Ltd, Aylesbury, Bucks.

CONTENTS

	Introduction	1
1	The Boys of Summer	5
2	Playing the White Man	109
3	The Wonderful and the Weird	131

INTRODUCTION

One of the problems with daily journalism is that theorising about it sends you bonkers. In the dusty back rooms of libraries, newspapers live forever. However, their contents have a half-life of about three hours between breakfast and elevenses. Next day, they are filling dustbins, lining cat litter trays and wrapping chips – though this last practice seems to be dying away, presumably, given the filth that most papers print these days, on grounds of public hygiene.

Journalists live with the fact that the stories they sweat over on Monday are forgotten by Wednesday. Quite often, this is rather a comfort. You can put aside past disasters and concentrate on doing better next time. Unfortunately, the stories you most wish to forget are the ones which end with some rotter suing for libel. But just occasionally, newspapers do print things that might be remembered a little longer. Since television has not yet got around to running old copies of *The Guardian* instead of midnight movies, a book is a pretty nice substitute.

I don't know whether anything in this volume is really worth a re-run though it is flattering that the publishers think so. Sports journalism is usually regarded as the lowest form of a low art, the ephemeral pursuit of the trivial, but in this form it acquires a certain cachet. Books are somehow more respectable than papers. Journalists are ruffians; authors are posh. *The Guardian* is very useful for lighting fires yet book-burning is regarded as sacrilege. When my first book was published four years ago my Mum, bless her, would

1

wander into shops and quietly shift the odd copy from a back shelf onto the display counter. She never does that at the newsagent.

What follows is a selection of almost 10 years' work from *The Guardian*. I was employed by the paper in 1979 as a sports sub-editor. The editor was, I believe, impressed that as a student I had been on a conducted tour of the old Manchester Guardian building in Cross Street. He then lectured me sternly on the importance of sports sub-editing and how I would not be allowed to spend my time doing anything fancy, like writing. I took the job, and a pay cut, on the off-chance that it would be possible to change his mind. By extreme good fortune I happened to arrive just as the great John Arlott was retiring and a vacancy was opening up for a junior cricket writer. Two years later I was the actual cricket correspondent, a job for which I would have donated a small limb some time earlier. It was widely said that I helped my case by being a notably idle and incompetent sub, but I have never gone along with this theory myself.

The cricket job meant that I was present at a number of the most important sporting events of the decade and the first half of the book is, in part, a reflection of that. However, between whiles, I have also reported something like 60 other sports for *The Guardian* and have been present at some of the least important sporting events of the decade as well. These get their place in the third section of the book.

I have refrained from including any of my efforts in seven years' reporting before joining *The Guardian* although I wrote copiously on Northamptonshire cricket for the evening paper, the *Chronicle and Echo*, and then reported on dozens of subjects for hundreds of papers while working for the sports desk at Reuters. This decision was taken partly on the grounds of quality control and partly because I can't find the cuttings. But I have always been lucky enough to work for a succession of sports editors – David Jones at Northampton, Clare McDermott and Steve Parry at Reuters, John Samuel and Mike Averis at *The Guardian* – who have tolerated, humored, and encouraged me. I am grateful to them. It is not their fault I still don't know the difference between 'that' and 'which'.

Here then is a rather patchy and idiosyncratic sporting history of the 1980s. It is a selection of those pieces of which I am least ashamed. One of my quirks as a writer is a habit of cross-referring to some other event of the day, which is possibly a subconscious means of trying to prove that I am not a complete fool and do read a the non-sporting part of the paper. I have either put footnotes to these, which is clumsy, or cut them out, which is cheating slightly, but was essential in those cases where I could no longer work out what I was talking about.

I trust these pieces still have some value. I am afraid this volume probably does not have much future wrapping chips, if only because it is the wrong shape. But in an emergency, and I am thinking here particularly of *Guardian* readers, it could be used as a substitute for pitta bread and filled with felafel.

Matthew Engel

1

THE BOYS OF SUMMER

On a Spring Bank Holiday Monday in 1980, *The Guardian* tentatively sent out the newish boy on the sports desk to cover a county game at Lord's. I was very excited. Two years later, I was on the plane to Australia, even more excited, newly-appointed as the *Guardian* cricket correspondent.

Five years after that, I gave up, suffering from ennui, angst, weltschmerz and giardisis, three mild disorders of the brain and one of the stomach. The mid-1980s for me were spent watching cricket round the world, and above all travelling from one cricket ground to the next. I visited every major cricketing stadium except Georgetown and, so it seemed, most of the airports, hotels and telex offices. In 1986 I spent eight months staying in hotels and on the 1986-87 tour of Australia there were 32 plane journeys. They were great years and I enjoyed them hugely but it is possible to have too much of even a very good thing. I am still reporting cricket but a little less obsessively; it has become something like fun again.

This section is culled from the million-plus words I have written on cricket in the paper in that period. It begins with that Bank Holiday game, a report which includes a reference, not entirely flattering, to the Middlesex fast bowler Mike Selvey. It concludes with an account of David Gower's batting at Lord's in 1989, a match I attended in the role of columnist, sitting alongside the self-same Selvey, by now my successor as cricket correspondent. It is not an outcome either of us would have dared bet on in 1980.

Most of that time was spent chronicling the long-running soap opera of the England team, sub-titled in this period The Darling Duds of May. I reported a dozen Test series, of which England won four and lost eight. I have included samples of both triumph and disaster. Some of the judgements on the triumphs erred on the optimistic side, but on the whole I think I made an effort to treat both imposters just the same.

Interspersed amongst the Test match pieces are accounts of some of the more dramatic one-day games of the era; county games, most of them chosen because they bring back happy memories for me; some 'think pieces', in which the thoughts may or may not still have some validity; and a number of oddities, most of which seem to involve Geoffrey Boycott. These include the reports of the occasion when the two of us contrived to get arrested at Trinidad airport.

I have tidied up the odd bit of grammar and cut one or two paragraphs of routine run-of-play and team news, the service information that has to be included in a daily report but is a bit tedious a few years later. I have preserved one *Guardian* misprint, which explains itself eventually. Other errors are accidental.

CRUEL SEA FOR SUSSEX

May 1980

The sun shone for much of the day, which was unexpected and pleasant. It is unlikely that Sussex noticed. They seem, at present, to be carrying the sea fret around with them, like Wellington in The Perishers who has his own personal rain cloud. Yesterday they lost to Middlesex at Lord's by an innings and five runs and, worse, lost Peter Graves, their most experienced batsman, with a broken finger.

Graves was hit twice, once by Daniel and once by Van der Bijl. He carried on, more courageously than we realised, but eventually sent a rising ball straight to third slip with a curious self-preserving shot that he would not have played normally. Graves has been through this before; he has broken his left forefinger twice, both times batting against Middlesex. This time, for an unpleasant change, it was his right forefinger. He will be out for about a month.

Sussex were already without their captain, Long, who was hit on the head by Daniel on Saturday. They have yet to win a game in either championship or Sunday League, have lost vast sums of money over the past two seasons, are employing three well-paid overseas players even though they can only field two at a time, and there are rumours of rebellion among the members. Apart from that, everything is fine.

Under the circumstances, Sussex did not play badly. Parker stayed three and a half hours for 43 before being last out. He has not scored many runs this season and looked out of form. Indeed, he got slower as the innings wore on, scoring only 11 in the last two hours; but he remained there in spite of himself, which is the mark of a good player and all that Sussex could have asked.

Selvey, the most sedate of the Middlesex fast bowlers, ended the long stand which Parker shared with Phillipson. This was a strange dismissal. Selvey hit Phillipson on the pad, appealed at once and got no response. Meanwhile, the ball had been taken by Gatting at forward short leg and he appealed for a bat-pad catch. Dickie Bird thought for several seconds before giving him out. The rest happened very quickly. From 132 for four, Sussex (minus Long) fell to 146 all out and Middlesex were home with maximum points.

THE QUICK KILL
June 1980

Northamptonshire reached the final of the Benson and Hedges Cup yesterday when they beat Middlesex by 11 runs at Lord's to end a match that veered from one side to the other half-a-dozen times and was, perhaps, one of the best one-day cricket matches ever played. Technically, of course, one-day is not quite right. The players reassembled yesterday for the last 14 overs – but even this brief passage produced a couple of fascinating twists. The game, which restarted in balance, swung first towards Middlesex, when they scored 29 in three overs, and then, dramatically and irrevocably, back to Northamptonshire as Sarfraz took three wickets in seven balls followed by the winning catch, a difficult swirling skier. The match award went to Williams for his resourceful batting and bowling.

Very few were around to watch. This was understandable. Employers can be suspicious about grandmothers' funerals that last into a second day; anyway, not many people would hang about to catch the last act of Hamlet if they had to endure an 18-hour interval and an umpire's inspection of the stage. The Tavern rowdies had gone, the phantom whistler had gone; loyally, the NW8 seagulls stayed behind to act as chorus.

The tactical battle between Brearley and Watts, two of the most experienced captains in the business, remained highly sophisticated. Brearley, whose team began the day needing 79 to win with five wickets left, could do little more; Watts had to pick the opportune moment to bring back his opening bowlers, Sarfraz and Griffiths, who were entitled to just two more overs each. Watts stuck with the spinners. The batsmen began watchfully. Then Van der Bijl, who is the thick end of seven feet tall and built like a block of St John's Wood flats, hit two sixes off successive overs, not slogs but almost languid pick-ups.

Nine overs to go, 46 wanted. No more wickets down. Now would Sarfraz come on? No, Watts opted for his own bowling, sturdy medium-pacers which steadied his team and the scoring rate. Then Willey bought Van der Bijl's wicket; or, rather, Van der Bijl bought it, since it was a fighter pilot's death, down in flames on the mid-wicket boundary.

Forty needed off seven, 27 off five, Gatting and Gould going well. Now, Sarfraz returned. His fourth ball took out Gould's off-stump. In the next over, he got Emburey as Sharp ran back to take a difficult catch. Gatting, by then on 91, recaptured the strike, swung across the line and was bowled.

This time, there were no further twists. Selvey had a last, despairing fling at Griffiths and Sarfraz snaffled it, running back from square cover. His team-mates mobbed him football style – a win by Northamptonshire over Middlesex at Lord's has something of the flavour of a Northampton Town win over Arsenal, even in these days of cricketing egalitarianism. This was Middlesex's first defeat in anything this season; it took a good team to beat them and Northamptonshire will grace the final.

SICK MEN OF THE MIDLANDS
May 1981

Good health is a mixed blessing in Nuneaton; you feel so out of things. Swapping medical stories is a local obsession. 'Ooh,' said a woman outside Marks and Spencer, 'our Elsie's legs are covered in blotches.' She seemed very proud.

The Warwickshire team are more reticent about their ailments, partly because it's hard for them to keep up to date. The all-rounder, Asif Din, yesterday became the fifth player to get Warwickshire's own private virus. Smith, the opener, may not bat today. The doctor more or less said that the

9

others will be all right if they avoid doing anything silly, like playing cricket.

They are battling on, but it is hard going. Kent already lead by 249 and have nine second-innings wickets left. The two declarations so far have come earlier than they might have done but, with these short boundaries. Asif Iqbal is unlikely to take chances with the third.

Warwickshire declared at tea, 106 behind, immediately after losing their seventh wicket and giving Kent a point, which puzzled many people. But I think Willis had worked out the possibilities carefully: the slim prospect of his sick men making a hefty fourth innings target against the slimmer one of their longish tail squeaking another batting point.

Between coughs and wheezes. Amiss and Lloyd had played some pleasant strokes; Humpage, the wicket-keeper whose batting approach is increasingly reminiscent of John Jameson, some powerful and obviously healthy ones. His 58 was top score. There was nothing in the wicket for the fast bowlers but just a little for the medium-pacers and spinners and both Woolmer and Johnson made good use of it.

In the evening, Woolmer batted well, stroking the ball with his old unhurried class, and he should reach a century this morning. It was his 33rd birthday and he seemed to spend most of the day smiling. One assumes he was just pleased with cricket and life; if he came from Nuneaton, though, it would probably mean he had a lovely cold coming on.

DAMP DAY AT DARTFORD
May 1981

There had not been a proper day's cricket in the south-east for nearly a fortnight;[1] one reacted to the rumour that they might play at Dartford rather like a Muscovite who hears a shop across town has acquired a consignment of Scotch or bananas: with disbelief and hope, and a powerful feeling that by the time one arrived it would be too late.

There was cricket, an hour and a half of it, between 3 o'clock and shortly after tea, when the thundery clouds that had thoughtfully skirted the ground all afternoon changed direction and steamed in. Kent put in to bat on a green but not especially unpleasant wicket, found time to reach 53 for one.

The chairman of selectors, Alec Bedser, was present. It was a good match for him to choose since almost half the participants are plausible candidates for the one-day internationals next week, including Love, the Yorkshire batsman who has been scoring runs as though it were going out of fashion, which it seems to be. The only batsmen for Bedser to view were Woolmer, Rowe and, briefly, Tavare, and for much of the time Woolmer must have craved privacy. He took 37 minutes to score a run and went from one to five with a chance that went via Bairstow's fingertips to the boundary. In fact, there were two separate games going on: Old regularly worrying and occasionally beating Woolmer at one end, Rowe consistently clipping Stevenson through the on-side at the other.

However, the scorebook will not reflect this. Mark Johnson, Yorkshire's burly recruit, replaced Stevenson and soon had Rowe playing on – his first championship victim, Woolmer survived and improved, eventually playing one handsome square-cut that may have had him looking up to make sure that Bedser had not gone home. Soon, the rain sent everyone home. Another day, another dolour.

[1] As in most Mays of the 1980s, the weather in May 1981 was wretched.

HAIL THE LORD OF LORD'S
July 1981

It was clear that if Surrey were going to prevent Somerset winning the Benson and Hedges Cup final on Saturday, they would have to get Vivian Richards out cheaply, which in his case means for less than 50. The last shot of the match, which was swallowed by the onrushing crowd, was assumed to be a four, and that took Richards to 132 and Somerset to their third one-day trophy in three years. QED.

There is little point in using adjectives to describe Richards' innings; they have all been devalued by overuse on lesser men. Some of his strokes, and I would single out one almighty pull off Thomas, were made with the air of a man sending a smelly kipper back to the kitchens. Take it away! Not fit for superhuman consumption. This was Richards' 26th innings in this competition and his first century. Maybe that is not so surprising. Somerset had never reached the final before and Richards is not your man for a damp day in late April against Minor Counties (West) at Amersham. But at Lord's he has triumphed again and again: in the County championship as well as in last year's Test and the World Cup and Gillette Cup finals of 1979.

Joel Garner's record is just as remarkable. In the three Cup finals in which Richards has scored centuries, Garner has taken 16 wickets. This time he took five for 14. The 14 may even be more significant than the five. For the first hour Surrey, put in to bat, could hardly hit the ball off the square – just 18 runs came off the first 18 overs and, though only two wickets were down, Surrey were already in deep trouble. However, they recovered quite well. Knight, front-footing as well as ever, had to play more uppish and chancy shots than he might have done in ideal circumstances but he kept finding the gaps until, aiming towards mid-wicket, he was caught by the wicket-keeper where fourth slip might have been, for 92.

It was unfortunate that a batsman of Roope's ability did not appear until six overs from the end, as No 8, but the final total of 194 did not look indefensible. It looked even better when Rose and Denning were out in the first three overs. Richards, offered the light by the umpires, having scored a less-than-confident 13, had no hesitation about marching off to the pavilion.

But when he came back, it was different. There was nothing much Surrey could do, given the use of the inner circle that stopped Knight putting everyone on the boundary for Richards, though it was surprising that he did not try to bring back Clarke before the 33rd over when Somerset were clear and away at 125 for three.

The only further wicket Surrey got was that of Roebuck, who made 22 out of a third wicket stand of 105, being mainly seen and not heard. When Botham came in, he naturally felt obliged to compete for attention. The closing stages were just a whacking session, 48 runs off the last 27 balls, and Somerset won with more than 10 overs to spare.

THE FASTEST WAITER IN WORCESTER
July 1981

Some people are just born unlucky. Hartley Alleyne was born in Barbados, the only place on earth where there is no shortage of very good and very fast bowlers. If he were English, he would spend his life playing Test cricket; instead he plays for Worcestershire and works between whiles as a waiter. Yesterday, however, glory beckoned at Lord's. He had taken eight Middlesex wickets for 43 on Saturday, including Emburey and Merry with the last two balls. When the champions started their second innings, 237 behind, he was even more lethal.

The first ball, a yorker, took Barlow's middle stump and gave Alleyne a delayed-action hat-trick. The fifth trapped Radley leg-before as he shuffled gingerly back. Middlesex were nought for two: it seemed that nothing could save them from an innings defeat. Then, in Alleyne's fourth over, Roland Butcher straight drove. Alleyne interrupted his follow through to try and stop it and slumped to the ground, 10 minutes before he was taken off on a stretcher. One feared the worst; the word from the dressing-room was that he definitely had a twisted ankle and a mournful look – it will be this morning before a firmer diagnosis can be made.

There was no more Alleyne and only one more wicket; Middlesex finished on 209 for three, with a chance not only of saving the match but even of winning. Their revival was simultaneous with England's. Perhaps Brearley can do things even more mysterious than quoting Jung.[1]

Butcher started it. He plays at such an astonishing pace that one wonders how an essentially sedate game like cricket ever attracted him. He would have been a world-beating greyhound. It took just 32 minutes (allowing for injury time) for Butcher to get his third 50 in three days; he then pulled Pridgeon for six, paused for breath then reached 66 and was stumped, the most appropriate way for him to go. Slack and Tomlins stayed till the close and Slack scored 110 not out. A Butcher century would have been more spectacular but always looked less likely. Slack, who came to Middlesex via St Vincent and Buckinghamshire, has always had a lot of good shots and this season has many fewer bad ones.[2]

Earlier, Middlesex had suffered in step with their captain at Headingley, but in the field. Scott, straight and unflinching, scored his sixth 50 since entering county cricket six weeks ago. Humphries made one too and Worcestershire scored 345.

The Lord's seagulls hovered as though expecting Middlesex blood; one made as if to dive-bomb a lady in the Warner Stand. They are getting noisier and cheekier. By next year they will be throwing cushions and trying to get in the pavilion without a tie.

[1] This match coincided with a rather more famous one between England and Australia at Headingley.
[2] Slack went on to score 248, the highest of his tragically curtailed career.

SOMERSET'S NEW EDWARDIANS
August 1981

Somerset beat Yorkshire by 167 runs halfway through the summer's afternoon at Abbeydale Park yesterday. It was not a surprising result. Yorkshire had already lost five matches this season and their immediate response to the challenge of scoring 353 for victory was to lose four wickets for 35. It was, however, a historic one. Somerset beat Yorkshire away twice in a row in 1901 and 1902 – famous wins, they were too – but had never managed it in the championship in the four reigns since. One wonders if Yorkshire's impregnable days will ever come again.

The Edwardian reminiscence is especially apt because the whole day seemed to evoke a lost England – only a few houses in sight dotted amid the wooded hills, only a few clouds dotted amid the blue sky and the big crowd (15,000 over the three days) with nothing better to do than watch county cricket. Abbeydale is in modern, sprawling Sheffield, geographically, but not spiritually.

Somerset batted on for a while yesterday then gave Yorkshire 310 minutes to win the match. They lost it in under an hour – Dredge dealing with Moxon and Athey (both lbw to balls that kept low) and Marks with Sharp and Hartley. Sharp was unlucky. He played quite a firm shot, but the ball kicked back onto his wicket. Hartley, who lost his middle stump, was not.

Love and Bairstow counter-attacked which is in their nature. Love looked high class, as he did early in the season, while Bairstow was irrepressibly Bairstow. They put on 102 in 27 overs, but the stand always looked like a diversion rather than a genuine threat to Somerset. Love, like Sharp, went oddly, the ball descending from glove to bails, Bairstow went more predictably, trying to drive into the distance and instead sand-wedging the ball to mid-on.

Love made 51 and Bairstow 70, Dredge skipped through the tail, finishing with six for 43: his best ever. He has an ungainly style and runs up as though playing Grandmother's Footsteps. He can be very effective on a wicket like this one, giving just a little help. Johnson was unable to bat after pulling a hamstring. For some weeks he will be in the Yorkshire Absentee XI, who currently look stronger than the actual team.

In the circumstances, it was not that bad a peformance by Yorkshire. It would have been a very even match had it not been for one sensational innings on Monday by Vivian

Richards. For a variety of reasons, a man from Antigua would not have been playing county cricket in 1902.

TIM LAMB LIGHTS THE FINAL PATH
August 1981

In a murky half-light and an atmosphere close to hysteria even among those who were sober, Northamptonshire beat Lancashire by one wicket with one ball of the final over remaining to reach the final of the NatWest Trophy, their third one-day final in successive years. Northamptonshire, chasing 187 for victory, lost their ninth wicket with 13 runs still needed. That brought in Jim Griffiths, regarded as a batting rabbit almost of Watership Down proportions, to join Tim Lamb, no Bradman himself, to face Holding, Allott and the near-darkness.

Nearly all the runs came in singles, many of them leg byes, but there were more mid-wicket conferences than anything else, or possibly lectures, as Lamb tried to advise Griffiths and protect him from the strike. He even turned down five easy singles. The finish was made even weirder by a five-minute hold-up at the start of the last over that must have baffled everyone except those who could hear the umpire, Alan Whitehead, asking the scorers which team had scored faster over the first 30 overs, a fine point that would have decided the match had the teams finished level on 186 for nine.

Lamb was made man of the match by Jim Parks, who admitted he had only made his decision after the final run was scored. Lamb had bowled extremely well and was partly responsible for Lancashire's collapse after lunch, with a spell of three wickets for two when Lancashire went from 116 for one to 161 for nine at bewildering speed. But one suspected the batsmen were more responsible than anyone else – there were some very panicky strokes in that period.

Lancashire's final total was made a little more respectable by a good last-wicket stand of 25 between Simmons and

Holding. But 187 was considerably less than Northampton-shire had made batting second in both their previous rounds. The wicket was easy paced and they began with some assurance. However, the absence of Willey, whose attempts to play with a broken thumb had failed, was a blow. And when Williams, who recovered from a rocky start to score 41, and Allan Lamb were out in successive overs to make the score 97 for four, Northamptonshire's reputedly powerful batting side started to look a good deal more vulnerable.

There was a stand of 53 between Yardley and Willey's deputy, Carter, and the game shifted back towards Northamptonshire. But with the light getting worse and worse – the game was kept going for public relations purposes rather than cricketing ones – Northamptonshire themselves collapsed, setting up the memorable finale.

LLOYD PILES ON THE AGONY
September 1981

A headline in yesterday's *Yorkshire Post* read simply: 'Supporters Unhappy.' It might have been a story about Yorkshire cricket or any of the local football teams. It turned out to be a report on angling in Barnsley. It was still an appropriate motif for the second day of the 211th Roses match.

Yorkshire, equal 10th in the County championship, had a thoroughly miserable time at Headingley against Lancashire, who are 16th. It was terminated only when an overcast day turned darker still and the last 100 minutes were lost to bad light. That did not make the supporters any happier though it did remove the possibility of Yorkshire losing in two days. They finished yesterday 46 for two in their second innings, still 151 runs behind. That gap can almost wholly be explained by an innings of 145 from Clive Lloyd, who far from adhering to the nonsense about no fours before lunch in these matches, struck a number of savage sixes.

Lloyd made it a thoroughly worthwhile day's cricket. But the Roses lived up to expectations in other ways. The old men sat in the football stand as one was told they did, wearing mackintoshes and lugubrious expressions, applauding knowingly and saying nowt. The trouble was there were so few of them. The crowd was about 4,000, which would never have done. But in the past the match never had to compete with a Test on television and the other untold delights of a modern August Monday. Next year, the game will end its link with the Bank Holiday and revert to the start of the month, which may help if there is any weekend left without a Test match.

Lloyd came in with Lancashire 79 for five, still 70 behind and his innings was not typical: it occupied only three hours in all and for an innings played at that speed included some surprisingly long thoughtful periods, particularly when Stevenson and Sidebottom were giving him something worth thinking about. But these were interspersed with brief hyperactive periods in which Stuchbury in particular found his bowling hooked and pulled with extraordinary power into the empty spaces of the terracing. All the bowlers suffered to some degree.

It was Lloyd's 37th birthday though I doubt if he was celebrating. Professional sportsmen with creaky knees do not take much pleasure from 37th birthdays. Pesonally, I have every confidence in Lloyd's ability to celebrate his 47th in the same way. But really he was celebrating the occasion. Lloyd could not enjoy tormenting Yorkshire more if he had changed his birthplace to Rawtenstall by deed poll. It was his third successive August Bank Holiday century against Yorkshire and his fifth in all, as many as Geoff Pullar, more than any of Cardus' heroic figures from the heroic age of this fixture.

Hughes and Simmons batted well enough to take the Lancashire first innings to 346. But it was still not an easy wicket, as the Yorkshire batsmen soon discovered. Love was bowled by Holding with one that kept unspeakably low. Lumb though was brilliantly caught, when David Lloyd stuck out his left hand more in despair than hope after a firm, low legside flick and found the ball lodged in it.

FINAL TO ECLIPSE THEM ALL

September 1981

Just as 1976 is remembered as the summer English weather went crazy, 1981 will forever be remembered as the summer English cricket went crazy. We dared and defied the first NatWest Trophy final to match the theatricals of the semi-finals and the Test series. And somehow it did.

We have seen similar things before, especially this season. But not like this, not in a final, not at Lord's – Cook the fielder and Miller the batsman racing each other to the stumps of the last ball, all but sending each other flying; the result in doubt until umpire Palmer at the bowler's end, realising that Constant at square leg was going to keep his finger to himself, signalled a leg bye before fleeing the mob.

Derbyshire beat Northamptonshire on the technicality of losing fewer wickets in a tied match, the way they won their semi-final, and Barry Wood became the first captain to hold up the new trophy, an ugly bit of metal compared to the old Gillette Cup. It looks more suited to bashing people over the head. And if Northamptonshire were allowed to lay their hands on it, that is probably what they would do to themselves.

Cook and Larkins gave them a grand start. In four rounds of the NatWest, their opening stands have been 111, 139, 124 and, this time, 99, with Larkins playing the more exhilarating shots but Cook having the resources to stay on for a century. It was enough to earn him the man of the match award from Viv Richards, conceivably even enough to get him in the tour party,[1] and certainly should have been enough to settle the contest. On an easy wicket, all Derbyshire could do was bowl straight, field well and hope for the best.

They were helped by a couple of marginal decisions – Cook's lbw for 111 and Allan Lamb's run-out – and some very indifferent Northamptonshire middle order batting. What should have been a near-impossible 270 to win became 236, still one more than any team batting second has made for victory in the 28 previous Lord's finals.

Derbyshire knew they were dependent on their two

overseas batsmen. Wright and Kirsten obliged with a second-wicket stand of 123 in 33 overs, playing the most assured strokes of the match – Kirsten the right-hander was particularly impressive – but not quite quickly enough. With 20 overs left, Derbyshire still needed six an over, a rate that stayed constant for quite a time. But then they began to lose wickets. After Barnett was out at the start of the third last over, 23 were wanted. The light was awful, the crowd were *in extremis*, Northamptonshire appeared to have the edge.

Then Sarfraz, who had just served up a full toss for Miller to smack for six, bowled two successive bad balls, a widish one and an inviting half-volley, both despatched by Tunnicliffe for four. Derbyshire were back in front of the game before the final ball, knowing – from happy experience – that a single to tie would be enough.

There never were such times: for Derbyshire, whose first trophy in 45 years comes after a season in which they have suffered more resignations than an Italian government; or for Wood, who in his Lancashire days was regarded as a total non-starter for captaincy, yet has transformed Derbyshire in less than two months by sheer enthusiasm as much as anything else.

For now, just one spoilsport thought. If Nottinghamshire, as seems likely, become champions next week then every one of the first class counties will have won a trophy in the 13 seasons since 1969. In some respects, that is very good for the game. But you will recall from childhood that the fairground stalls that offered every kid a prize invariably had the least worthwhile prizes.

[1] True.

EXIT THE MASTER OF A DYING ART
September 1981

To the accompaniment of the warmest ovation a small crowd could manage, the Surrey team stood back after lunch yesterday and let their oldest, baldest and best-loved player lead them onto The Oval pitch. The end of the 1981 season is also the end of Intikhab Alam's career in first class cricket. The retirement of a great player is always a sad occasion. But Surrey will find Inti more than normally irreplaceable: as one of cricket's great charmers, as an overseas player (they are not allowed to import another) and, above all, as a leg-spinner.

Inti's career with Surrey has outlasted Robin Hobbs' with Glamorgan by a matter of days. There are no more high class leg-spinners left and none are in sight. The mould has been broken. This obituary may be premature. There is just a chance that Inti's family business (T-shirts and sports gear) back in Pakistan will be less demanding than he thinks, and that he will squeeze in another season or so. But it is a remote chance.

There was even a report yesterday that Robin Hobbs would now join Surrey (a Hobbs playing for Surrey again, there's a thought). Both men have done well this year; Inti, in particular, has benefitted from the hard and bouncy wickets at The Oval – 65 wickets this year, nearly 1,600 in all. He'd love to come back but he'll be 40 in December. Best to get out, he feels, when you're winning.

'It's very sad what's happened to the leg-spinner,' said Inti yesterday. 'India and Pakistan are still producing them. But there's no incentive in English cricket. Everything's so financial, so competitive. A young leg-spinner needs time and a very, very good captain. You also need constant practice. As a kid, I used to get into the nets at two in the afternoon and bowl until six. I'd curse and say "Give me batting," and they would say, "No, you bowl." And it was the only way to learn. There just aren't the facilities for that in England.

'Of course the wickets don't encourage you either. But I do hate some of the stuff I hear. "It's a green wicket, so you can't bowl," or "It's a slow wicket, so you can't bowl." If you are a bowler, you should bowl on anything.'

Between the wars Inti would have done. In 1928, 'Tich' Freeman of Kent took 304 wickets. Of all the feats of yesteryear, I find that the hardest to believe. And Freeman was a leg-spinner. 'Every ball he tossed into the air,' wrote Cardus, 'was an alluring problem to batsmen and spectators alike; a sinuous curve, a floating enticement, a hovering invitation – "Please drive me, I am a half-volley." Then a swoop downwards, a spin of a top, and the rest is silence – interrupted by the call of the wicket-keeper for a catch or a stumping.'

And so it almost was at The Oval yesterday. For an hour Inti waited at mid-on and third man, with just an occasional flex of the arm in case Knight, his captain, had forgotten him; then the nod of recognition from Knight, an appreciative murmur from the pavilion, and the little sideways run-up.

Inti's second ball was tossed high, like a shuttlecock. Another was almost turned past the outside edge of Brian Hardie's bat. Eventually Keith Fletcher did receive one of those hovering invitations, which he accepted: four runs, past mid-off. And Inti smiled and thought the traditional leg-spinner's thought: there is always the next ball. Now there is not even that.

LAMB TANS THE RHINO'S HIDE
July 1982

There was a moment around midday at Trent Bridge on Saturday with Pakistan 100 for none and proceeding at full tilt when, for the first time since the May-Willis regime began, the England cricket team looked in danger of falling apart. Hours later, when England had won the first one-day international by seven wickets – and an easy seven wickets at that – it was hard to remember what on earth one had been worried about.

Pakistan, who looked as though they might score 300 or more, finished with 250 for six. England knocked off the runs with nearly eight overs to spare. Allan Lamb scoring 118 to be man of the match and, towards the end, one's only concern was what enormity the dafter spectators might perpetrate next.

We had better avoid animal analogies for them. It is fair to say, though, that Pakistani teams have in the past shared some of the characteristics of the rhinoceros, a formidable-looking beast which starts to charge with devastating intent but instead of reaching its target tends to stop dead, run straight past or disappear at a tangent having forgotten what it was trying to do in the first place. There was something of this in the way this Pakistan team frittered away the glorious start given them by Mudassar and Mohsin. But the positive side was the way England, having performed very moderately with the new ball, turned the game round with effective back-up bowling (Hemmings' figures did not reflect a most encouraging debut) and magnificent fielding.

England's batsmen lived up to their typecasting. Tavare looked awful but got runs. Gower, given the opener's job in preference to Randall, looked good but got out. Lamb looked great *and* made runs in a style that was orthodox in every respect except the intent with which he made them. He later remarked that he was not entirely happy with his form; he thought his grip might be wrong.

Pakistan had an impossible time bowling to him, wrong grip or not. Imran caused a lot of trouble at first but had no one to replace him – certainly no equivalent of Hemmings – and there was a triple blow when Sarfraz dropped Lamb in the deep. Lamb stayed in with devastating effect, Sarfraz injured his hand and went off for 20 minutes and, under the new rules, could not bowl for a further 20 minutes, which wrecked Imran's timetable.

For the second game today, the Old Trafford authorities would like the crowd to be as large but more intelligent. The Trent Bridge pitch was invaded six times and Lamb, when he did get out, had to dash to the pavilion. Phil Carling, the Nottinghamshire chief executive, said he had hired the normal number of police and the club would have to think long and hard to find a way of improving things. The policy of trying to segregate the crowd, football-fashion, did not seem much help. There was a large sign marking the 'Pakistani Enclosure', which I was discouraged from entering by a steward. What the three-man delegation from South Africa, where they have abolished that sort of thing, made of it, heaven only knows.

TITMUS POSTED IN
August 1982

It was supposed to be a day of departures; Mike Brearley was starting his last match at Lord's, and Surrey announced that they were releasing Graham Roope, who has played in 21 Test matches, one fewer than W. G. But some people depart more often than others. At 10.40 the 49-year-old sub-postmaster of Potten End, Hertfordshire, a Mr Titmus, popped his head round the door of the Middlesex dressing-room to say hello. Twenty minutes later he was playing.

In the evening, something even loopier happened. The Surrey seam bowler Kevin Mackintosh took what may or may not constitute a hat-trick: a spell that went wicket, wicket, no-ball, wicket. Between these two events, some pretty dreary cricket took place, Middlesex spending all day to reach 273 for eight.

Titmus had not so far appeared on the field, but we know he is playing. We have it on the authority of one of those po-faced Lord's announcements that brook no argument: Delete S. P. Hughes, insert F. J. Titmus. It shook everyone, though it was not quite in the class of the announcement made years ago, before the amateur distinction was abolished: Delete F. J. Titmus, insert Titmus, F. J.

Titmus officially retired in 1976 but has reappeared for a Final Farewell Tour every two years since, in the manner of Dame Nellie Melba – one game for Surrey in 1978, five for Middlesex in 1980. This time, he said, he was in town to get a visa for MCC's American tour and dropped by, to be greeted by Brearley with the words: 'Ah, just the man.' One wondered if this was a leg-pull, but Titmus stood there, 33 years after first playing county cricket, wearing Radley's flannels, Brearley's boots and a bemused look, swearing blind that he was as surprised as we were and only slightly less surprised than his wife, who was handing out the old age pensions when he rang to say he would be late back.

What was Brearley up to? Middlesex, remember, are playing both Emburey and Edmonds. Well, the wicket is secondhand and potentially rewarding for the spin bowler but sited so near to the Tavern that it might be chancy for the slow left-armer. The extra off-spinner could be handy. Furthermore, Surrey are stacked with the off-spinners' fancy: left-handed batsmen.

Surrey's lone spinner, Needham, did not do much yesterday, it must be said, but nor did the batsmen. Brearley spent nearly two and a half hours over 43; Slack five hours over 79. The run-rate was pathetic. However, Middlesex, with Leicestershire starting to chase them hard at the top of the table, desperately wanted a third batting point. So at last they began to slog.

When the 100th over started, five runs were still wanted. Radley got two off the first but was caught behind off the second. Edmonds came in, aimed a fierce hook at the next, toppled over and landed on his stumps. The hat-trick ball was a no-ball, but the next bowled Cowans. Mackintosh leapt in the air with delight and the assembled company debated whether it was a hat-trick or not. My feeling is that, technically, it must be.[1]

Meanwhile, the sub-postmaster had to get his pads on in a panic. In 33 years he can hardly have seen anything as strange as that. Middlesex never did get their bonus point; I trust everyone got their pensions.[2]

[1] Wrong, apparently.
[2] The real reason for Titmus' inclusion emerged sometime afterwards. Apparently Edmonds had turned up late.

ENGLAND SURRENDER TO LAWSON
December 1982

Adelaide: Since the zenith of Empire there have been countless occasions, on the cricket field as well as the battlefield, when smug English assumptions about the ease of the task in hand have been horribly disproved by events. There have been few disasters as swift, unexpected and utter as the one which hit England's cricket team yesterday.

In 70 extraordinary minutes of a boiling Adelaide afternoon (the watches of an English winter's night, with the BBC observing radio silence) the batting collapsed from 181 for three to 216 all out. In that time most of England's hopes of saving the third Test and the Ashes disappeared. The wicket was as easy as when Australia were in: only the quality of batting and bowling was different.

Following on, England finished at 90 for one, still 132 behind. Gower was batting comfortably at the close, which is what England were hoping for at the start, though they had other circumstances in mind. The waters had closed over the wreckage, everything was serene again and it was hard to realise that it really had all happened. Today is a rest day – or at any rate a day for convalescence.

How did it happen? On Saturday England had done a reasonable retrenchment job, restricting Australia to 438 when 500 was likely. Yesterday morning Lamb and Gower became the first pair of the series to bat through a full session. Once in a while one of the Australian fast bowlers would worry them with an exceptional ball or they would be too inclined to speculate to accumulate. But batting for the most part was very easy.

Bowling, on the other hand, was murder. The temperature was almost 100 (it stayed just below, perhaps in deference to those England batsmen who have a phobia about the figure), and that was in the shaded stands. The Australians went out after lunch with little to look forward to except tears, toil and sweat. Two balls later Gower was out. Like Taylor and Hemmings but none of the others, there was little he could do to stay in. Lawson produced a ball that climbed exceptionally fast and, though every instinct told Gower to get his bat out of the way, there was no time to obey.

Gower was out for 60 but, no matter, Lamb was still there, leonine, nearing his century in comfort and passing 700 runs for the tour. And Botham was batting in a most businesslike fashion. At 2.20 England were well on the way to doing everything that could reasonably be expected, given the initial errors of selection and toss and the growing evidence that they are the weaker side, towards saving the game. At 3.30

they were all out.

Lamb and Randall both went in one Lawson over. Lamb, on 82, tried to hook and was given out caught behind, departing with a hard-done-by look and the most perfunctory acknowledgement of the crowd's applause. One cannot be certain in these matters but the playback did suggest a woody sound. Randall could have no complaints. He played over and round a yorker, was hit on the boot and bowled. He was lucky he could be given out only once.

Miller went when Hogg replaced Lawson, shoving a pointless half-drive to gulley where Yardley juggled and held on. One fancied, as the drinks trolley came out, that it might really be a tumbril. But Botham was still batting soundly and there was plenty to come. Plenty began with Taylor, promoted above Pringle to play one of his safe good-old-Bob innings; he won England's last Test here with one. Yardley produced a ball that bounced a shade more than expected; caught at slip, 199 for seven and 40 still wanted to save the follow-on.

For a while Botham nursed Pringle. Then Thomson returned. His first ball, little more than a loosener, was turned by Botham to mid-wicket where Wessels leaned forward and caught it. There was a brief pause while everyone took in the implications. Then Botham, after 93 minutes and 35 runs, departed.

Thomson quickly whipped out Hemmings and Willis and, while he was still in the mood, had Tavare caught bat and pad in the second innings, making it four wickets in 19 balls. Tavare, who made one on Saturday, did not do quite as well this time. Since his long, long vigil at Perth he has made 24 in five Test innings.

Fowler, who in his three Tests has emerged as a second-innings specialist, stuck around with Gower and before long the Australian bowlers really were tired. The occasionals, Border and Hookes, came on and life was carefree again. In theory England could still save the game, but on this tour optimists go demented.

The crowd was again good, above 18,000, but not all as good as gold. Ten people were arrested and 46 ejected (compared to 14 and 80 on Saturday, when a policeman was concussed after being kicked in the head). One spectator yesterday was wearing a T-shirt saying on the front 'First class Yobbo' and on the back 'retired due to police harassment'. Retired or not, he was thrown out.

MILLER'S MAGIC MOMENT
December 1982

Melbourne: England won the fourth Test by three runs; it was the 250th Test match between England and Australia and only one (Manchester 1902) has produced as close a result. None can have matched this one in its combination of sustained fascination over four-and-a-bit days plus outrageous finish.

It had been a marvellous game when at 5.15 on Wednesday afternoon Thomson walked out to join Border, with Australia 74 runs behind and nine wickets down. England's victory merely awaited ratification. By 12.25 yesterday, when Botham bowled, Thomson edged towards the slips, Tavare fumbled and Miller held the catch, its place in the memory was secure. In two countries, half a planet apart but linked by this rather ludicrous pastime, millions of nerves were shot to pieces. Bob Willis said he was not worried in the least and that he always knew Botham would do it. There may be someone, somewhere, who believes him.

Had England lost, nothing in the remaining two months of the tour – the final Test starting in Sydney on Sunday and the one-day extravaganza that follows – could have stopped the whole enterprise from being damned forever as a failure, and Willis' captaincy with it. Now England can still keep the Ashes by winning in Sydney and squaring the series 2-2. And even if they fail, they can expect to emerge from this tour with some credit and hope. As Cowans (made man of the match after his six for 77) is now emerging as a possible spearhead of the attack for the foreseeable future, a new England who can win

Test matches without requiring Botham to act as an all-purpose superhero is beginning to take shape. 'We knew back home that Cowans had the skeleton to be a great fast bowler,' said Willis, 'but we had to put the flesh on that skeleton. It's been up and down at times but he's worked very hard. He's now reaping the fruits of that hard work.'

It is a shame to spoil such an occasion (when, by the way, was there ever such a congruent Test match, with all four totals within a 10-run band?) by cavilling about anything. But it was only a few minutes before someone suggested that the whole result might have been set up by the Channel Nine people to bump up the viewing figures for the Sydney Test, so there is no harm entering the odd little caveat.

The fact remains that just as Australia very nearly won the game, England very nearly lost it. Willis maintained the policy of offering Border singles, so that England could get at Thomson, almost until the end. And a very bitter end it might have been. Whether or not the plan was wrong in conception – and it was argued over at two team meetings, evening and morning – it almost failed in execution, because Border and Thomson were such sharp runners. Border took two-thirds of the strike.

There is not much time now either to worry about that or to savour the flavour of victory. The next Test begins in less than 48 hours and three England players are doubtful: Cook, Fowler and Randall. Losing one of these three is not an insuperable problem. Two missing can be coped with, too, now that Trevor Jesty is here, though if Cook and Fowler were both absent England would have to return to the game of hunt-the-opener. If all three were out, England would have to start considering the merits of Gould as a batsman. And, little ray of sunshine that he is, he did his chances no harm whatever with his performance as fielder and general gee-er-upper when he subbed for Fowler in this match.

The Sydney pitch may well give the spinners appreciable help, in which case Hemmings would probably replace Pringle, although Pringle, both as batsman and bowler, came out of this match with his reputation enhanced – like everyone else in the team. Only Gower was a complete failure and he ... (no, Willis declined to say anything about umpire Whitehead, so let's leave the subject alone) ... well, he has plenty of credit in the bank. With Border now back in favour, the Australians will probably field the same eleven.

Border was clearly the man of the morning. It was a grey day, but 10,000 people turned up prepared to see something for nothing even if it was only one delivery. In fact, there were 97. The first six overs were with the old ball, and in this period England managed the situation well. Cowans bowled three successive maidens, and Australia eked out only two runs and a leg bye.

Surely the new ball would finish them off. But, as England refused to attack Border, he began to forget that he was out of form. He found gaps to push singles and turn ones into twos. The total, 218 for nine when Thomson came in, 255 overnight, edged closer to the magic number of 292. The batsmen had to take risks, and England would have won more easily had they been less het-up. There would certainly have been a run-out had not an over-enthusiastic Lamb been in collision with a surprised Gould. Thomson played and missed three times and stepped away to leg to take singles, but everything worked for him. It began to look as though England themselves were about to be well and truly Headingley-ed.

The total passed 280 before Willis brought a man on to the square against Border. He promptly smashed a three through the covers and worked two down to fine leg. Australia were now within one boundary of victory. But a boundary was the one thing that England's policy had denied them all morning. And at the start of the 17th over of the day, Botham had Thomson where he wanted him, taking strike at the start of an over. The rest is cricketing history, and we will bore our grandchildren something dreadful.

LILLEE'S DYING LIGHT
June 1983

In the late afternoon sunlight on Saturday, Dennis Lillee and Jeff Thomson bowled together again, for the first time at Lord's since their reign of terror eight years ago. This time there were no English batsmen, their spirits broken by physical danger. Instead, there were the West Indians and Vivian Richards in particular. It is hard to believe this was the same sport.

West Indies beat Australia by seven wickets to make certain they would reach the semi-finals of the World Cup, which no one doubted. They only had 13 balls to spare at the end but for the last two hours or more this victory was not in doubt. The uncertainty was only whether Greenidge or Richards would reach their centuries. In the event, neither did: Greenidge got out for 90 and Richards, who regards Lord's centuries as his *droit de seigneur*, lost the strike to Lloyd at the crucial moment.

This was an occasion rather than a contest. Even if Australia had won, it would not have changed their prime task, which is to beat India today. Thus Lawson, who had a groin strain, did not play, though he practised merrily enough. But Lord's was jammed and everyone enjoyed themselves, with the exception of some of the bowlers.

This was true of both sides – the West Indies attack had less zip than in their three previous games (though Marshall was again exceptionally quick) and the catching was erratic. Hughes, Hookes and Yallop all scored 50s and Australia were able to get 273 for six. But on this mild pitch, against an Australian attack that offered little support to Rodney Hogg, this was not a target likely to bother the West Indians. Their batsmen all appear to be moving into prime form for the strategic moments this week, Richards (man of the match for the second time running) most of all.

There was a moment when Lillee produced a delivery of respectable line and length, which Richards no more than chivvied through mid-wicket for a certain four. More than most sportsmen, Lillee has raged against the dying of the light. But he seemed then to have a sudden look of serenity, of resigned acceptance. There are new fast bowling greats around, and the greatest of these is Marshall.

KAPIL SUBVERTS WORLD ORDER
June 1983

All manner of strange things happened at Lord's on Saturday, but the strangest probably came when Vivian Richards, who had been playing a game somewhere between cricket and a sophisticated form of clock golf, mis-hit an intended pull towards Father Time and was very well caught by Kapil Dev. The curiosity was not just that Richards was out, though that amazed everyone, not least Richards. It was that his dismissal did not signal, as usual, a retreat back into the bars but the reverse. It shook the crowd back to the realisation that India could win the Prudential World Cup, a possibility which had been eliminated from every mind for several hours. And at 7.28 – two minutes to midnight back home – they duly did, beating West Indies by 43 runs.

Midnight's children were deserved and decisive winners not just of the final, but of the whole fiesta. Within the past seven days, they have beaten Australia, England and West Indies with conviction and flair. The credit must go to brave, sensible and adaptable batsmen: spectacularly unspectacular bowlers helped by their own persistence and the soggy spring, which gave so many pitches a speed-deadening soft underbelly: and the rapidly improving captaincy of Kapil Dev. He outshone Lloyd by some distance in the final in his deployment of much sparser bowling resources.

India were 50 to 1 outsiders a fortnight ago, 100 to 1 with one gent in the Warner Stand between innings on Saturday (he is now £100 poorer); and heaven knows how many 1,000 to 1 when they were 17 for five against Zimbabwe at Tunbridge Wells the previous week. But the blunt fact is that the initial odds were not wrong. If the same personnel could be reassembled in the same circumstances another 50 times, India probably would not win again. It is a bit like the infinite number of monkeys at an infinite number of typewriters eventually writing *Hamlet*. And there were an infinite number of us typewriter-types feeling like monkeys on Saturday night.

It has to be said that, though the excitement was worthy of the occasion, much of the batting was not. India had a great deal of help from the vanquished. In detective fiction, it is always the unconsidered clue – the paint-stain on the trousers, the cigar-butt in the shrubbery – that turns out to be crucial. The outcome of the final was decided after India had made a pig's ear of the silk purse of a start given them by Srikkanth and Amarnath and collapsed from 90 for two to 130 for seven.

At this point, the crowd's attention started to wander. Lloyd would be holding up the trophy, just as in 1975 and 1979 except for his trendier specs and wobblier legs. Shall we have the chicken legs now or later? It seemed of no consequence that while Gomes was wheeling away, the last three wickets were adding 53. Even when Richards was batting – a drive to three o'clock, a cheeky flick to nine o'clock – people were admiring but hardly agog. It was just like any number of domestic Cup finals. Any news from Wimbledon?

Well, West Indian batsmen can get *hubris* like all other over-cocky conquerors. Greenidge did not play a ball he should have done and was bowled; Gomes and Bacchus made the reverse mistake; Lloyd, in pain after aggravating his groin injury, and Haynes both mis-drove. After 50 for one, it was 76 for six. But to the end there were possibilities. Dujon was reassuring in everything except his running. All the West Indian bowlers can bat, and three of them did so – Garner and Holding staying together for half an hour at the end until they had started to run out of overs as well as wickets. Had the target been much less than 183, West Indies would have won. Had it been much more, their batsmen would have been more prudent and would probably also have won.

Afterwards one captain criticised the wicket as too favourable to the seamers; the other disagreed. Surprisingly, it was Kapil Dev who was critical. Lloyd thought the pitch was perfectly fair and blamed his batsmen. Then he quietly announced his retirement from the captaincy.[1] All politics permitting, Richards will lead the 1984 West Indian party to England with Lloyd as his elder statesman.

The man of the match award – a worthy conundrum for Brearley's brain – went to Amarnath for all-round worthiness though Madan Lal cannot have been more than a short head behind. I would have gone for Kapil Dev, for bowling well, leading well, holding the Richards catch and as a symbol that India's triumph belonged to the team and indeed the nation.

India's triumph will obviously help the game there. It may not harm the West Indies either. The whole tournament has done English cricket good with much bigger average gates than in the previous World Cups, a total attendance of around 250,000 and profits of over £1 million, of which something like a half will stay in England. There would have been a far bigger profit if English cricket had an adequate stadium. The English authorities will tell the International Cricket Conference this week that, if they can have a bigger slice of the cake, they will gladly stage another in 1987. Perhaps if other countries took a turn, the world could even stand one every two years. India and Australia are keen. But if the Australians staged it, they really would have to stick to this format, which has both cricketing credibility and popular appeal, instead of lumbering the world with their pyjama rubbish.

One thing about the Australian one-day system, in which everyone plays everyone else *ad nauseam*, is that it is less likely to produce a shock result than this one. Perhaps now people outside India will be less free with the title 'world champions' than they have been during the West Indies' reign. But the shock will do us all good.

---

[1] He later un-retired.

ESSEX FLAP IN BLACK COMEDY
July 1983

The main problem watching cricket these days – apart from the strain 8.48 p.m. finishes impose on the eyes, newspaper deadlines and the patience of loved ones – is that one's flabber is constantly being gasted. Just four weeks after one astonishing Lord's occasion, on Saturday we saw the Son of World Cup Final. As is the way with remakes, the box office returns were a bit lower, the cast was more homespun and the plot even more far-fetched.

Almost throughout a very long day, Essex and everyone else assumed that they would regain the Benson and Hedges Cup. That went to Middlesex. Instead, Essex regained a title they hoped and believed they had lost for ever: that of cricket's champion foul-up merchants.

Middlesex won by four runs, with five possible balls remaining, after Norman Cowans had bowled Neil Foster with a delivery that was sharp enough to have done the business even in daylight. It was a considerable triumph for Middlesex and their new captain Mike Gatting. It was reasonable to assume that, after Brearley's retirement, the team might have to pause for consolidation. Instead they have won the first available trophy, one that eluded Brearley for 11 years.

But Essex's record as underachievers is even more extraordinary. In the 1970s they kept narrowly missing the Sunday League; twice recently they have lost semi-finals with the scores level because they had lost more wickets; in 1980 their batting collapsed to throw away the Benson and Hedges final; and last Wednesday, against Kent in the NatWest, they staged what turned out to be a dress rehearsal. Chasing 275, they were 210 for one and lost by the same tantalising four runs.

This time they only needed 197, and with 25 overs left were 127 for one. But despite the shortened boundaries that made Lord's look like Luton or Nuneaton, run-getting had never been easy, except during Gooch's brief and glorious ascendancy. The pitch seemed just sufficiently holding to prevent the ball coming freely on to the bat.

The Essex swing merchants tied Middlesex right down and Radley survived only by being quick-witted enough to break most of the customary rules of batsmanship including the law of averages (he might have been caught four times) on his way to 89 not out and the man of the match award.

The pattern changed only when Gooch was in. It was his 30th birthday. For most successful young businessmen that is a slightly disturbing milestone in the midst of a period of hope and expansion, past the uncertainties of youth and before those of middle age. For Gooch, it was a day back in the sunshine, a trusty prisoner's outing, before being locked back in obscurity. His sentence for collaborating with South Africa still has 21 months left to run.

He made the most of the occasion. Having bowled so well that Essex had no need to risk their sole spinner, Ray East, Gooch batted quite brilliantly. He took 16 off Cowans' opening over in a manner that must have reminded Cowans of Greg Chappell at Perth. In those circumstances, there is no such thing as a good-length ball. Cowans went out of the attack, though his revenge, which had to wait three Tests against Australia, was to come more swiftly this time. Gooch went on, driving imperiously on the up until, after taking 46 off 51 balls, he made his first mistake and departed.

Edmonds and Emburey now forced Essex to slow up, but since 71 had come off the first 10 overs, this hardly seemed relevant; the one worry was that Essex might be forced to wait until Monday. An hour had been lost in the morning as the weather reverted to its form of the early rounds of this competition. But golden July reasserted itself, the light held up well and at 6.16 the players trooped off for tea, or possibly cocktails.

However, even in this highest of high summers, there is a tendency for night to follow day. And as seven passed, and then eight, it got darker. To his credit, Fletcher did not moan about this later. He had won the toss and forced the Middlesex batsmen to endure the muggy morning. This was the reverse side of the coin.

And so the innings gradually got screwed down. McEwan

was caught at extra cover, Fletcher at silly point, Pont was hit by a bouncer from Williams and groggily dropped his bat on to the stumps. Then Hardie, who had hit five fours as Gooch's supporting act, but none in 29 overs later, was caught behind. The ride was getting turbulent but Pringle and Turner took over the controls. There was still no reason to suppose that Essex would not reach their destination.

With four overs to go and only 10 wanted, Pringle was lbw to Daniel. With 15 balls left, Turner tried to break free and was well caught by the substitute John Carr, son of Donald the TCCB secretary, who was making a suitably distinguished entry into the game's consciousness. The next ball went for four off the inside edge of David East's bat. Then Gatting caught him. The 54th over produced only a wide from Daniel and the running out of Ray East. Five were still wanted by the last pair, Foster and Lever, whose very presence one week after a major stomach operation was an act of slightly batty, very British heroism.

Then Cowans versus Foster and Cowans' triumph. Foster was furious with himself. But, on an individual level, he was one of the day's big winners. On his first major occasion, he bowled as though he were doing something natural, graceful and easy. This white hope is, I think, an authentic one. Lunatic cup finals are becoming commonplace; young fast bowlers like that are not.

FINAL DAY OF DELIGHT FOR THE CHEERFUL CHAMPIONS
September 1983

By degrees, through a Novemberish day at Chelmsford which confirmed the view that it was time cricket gave over, it became ever more certain that it would take witchcraft rather than Middlesex to stop Essex. At 4.20 that certainty became fact and, four years after the first and glorious Essex title, they became County champions for the second time, on the final day of the season and of Schweppes sponsorship.

37

The clincher was the news that the Middlesex game had been abandoned. It came through just after the Essex players had walked off in the drizzle, having bowled out Yorkshire and put themselves in what would have been a winning position, had the weather held. The game never resumed. But by then no one cared. The faithful – and Essex have plenty of them – massed in their macs outside the pavilion. The contrast between them and the loonies who stood in the same place cheering Yorkshire's Sunday League triumph two days earlier was startling. There was no cavorting. These were real old-fashioned cricket people. They waited and got wet until the Essex captain Keith Fletcher appeared on the pavilion steps to give an old-fashioned winner's speech, thanking the supporters, the players, the back room staff, the ground staff (especially them, a few cynics would add) and the supporters again. There were no Yorkshire people in evidence to note the melancholy fact that the greatest cricketing county of all had finished bottom for the first time ever.

This is the first time since 1977, the year Gloucestershire threw it away at the death, that the race has gone to the final day. In 1975, Leicestershire did not become champions until 15 September; that year the seasons got so mixed up that Chris Balderstone played in the final match against Derbyshire and for Doncaster Rovers on the same day. When Essex first won the title in 1979, it was all wrapped up on 21 August. It was a day later this year before they even hit the front. But the contest between them and Middlesex has been a good one, and healthy for cricket's most fragile but most enduring competition. The publicity might even inspire some firm to step in and sponsor it.

Perhaps Middlesex might have fractionally stronger hard luck stories. But Essex had injuries at critical times to Lever, Foster and Pringle. Their victory was a triumph for adaptability – often their later batsmen, like David East, got important runs, and for professionalism. Most times the early batsmen, and McEwan (who scored 2,176 in the season) in particular, got enough. But the player who did most for them was John Lever, a genuinely lionhearted cricketer who took

106 wickets, despite missing seven championship matches, in which time he had a serious stomach operation. Then, when Pringle and Foster were injured, Norbert Phillip came back from the verge of the sack to take 43 wickets in the last five weeks.

The two best ways to sour the generally cheery Essex atmosphere are to suggest that they doctor their pitches (if they were at it any more than other counties, they would probably do it more efficiently; only one of their 11 wins was at Chelmsford), and to tell Fletcher that the team is past it. Fletcher, who at 39, intends to keep playing for at least another year or two, believes the team will be better next year; though it is hard to see any replacement spin bowlers if Acfield and Ray East lose form.

The team that won this championship is almost identical to the 1979 team and all of them have been invited back next year. Ray East is to become captain of the Second XI in place of Mike Denness, who is leaving, but he will be available for the first team if needed.

The main surprise of the day was that Boycott failed to get his 2,000 runs. He was out in the second over still 59 short. The day's major batting performance came from his younger partner Moxon, who looked in pain even before he started getting hit regularly in the ribs as a result of the pitch's peculiarities. But he batted unflinchingly and, when he had the chance, drove handsomely. Until he was out for 58 Yorkshire were holding on well and, had the news from Nottingham been less reassuring, Essex might have got panicky. But Lever and Turner worked steadily through the rest. Essex would have needed 137 to win in 90 minutes, which might have been a good chase. But the rain was welcome now: and it can rain all it likes until April 1984.

UNLIKELY START TO A REVOLUTION
November 1983

The people who gathered in the Royal Baths, Harrogate did not look particularly touched, at least no more than the average for people who spend Sunday evenings listening to speeches in public halls. There were about 100 of them and the collection, it was announced to great applause, raised £72.33.

It might have been a meeting about almost anything, though it is unlikely that a casual passer-by would put the running of a cricket club high on the list of possibilities. And yet that is precisely what it was; the first local meeting held by the Yorkshire Members 1984 Committee, which next month will attempt to defeat and if possible unseat the official committee of the Yorkshire County Cricket Club, with a view to reinstating the glories of the past and, above all, Geoffrey Boycott.

One gets so inured to extraordinary occurrences in Yorkshire cricket that it is possible to miss the full bizarre nature of all this. My first thought on arrival was that it was like a political meeting, probably of the old-time Labour Party. At any moment I expected some dim eminence, who had once been under-secretary of something, to arrive, evade a few questions and dash back to the station. This political image became overwhelming as the night wore on.

We did not get an under-secretary. Indeed, there were no eminences at all; none of the committee members who voted to sack Boycott was present, or anyone else with much of a reputation within the game. Instead, we got Reg Kirk and Sid Fielden, who were introduced as 'the member for Hull' and 'the member for Doncaster.' Kirk and Fielden are the leaders of the pro-Boycott Tendency within the main Yorkshire committee. Their speeches contained few technical cricket terms. Instead, there were phrases like 'collective responsibility ... fellow traveller ... party line ... inner caucus'.

Boycott was not present either. He is carefully keeping his distance. But his spirit suffused the meeting as though his portrait had been hung above the podium. Someone even compared Boycott to Churchill and Michael Crawford, the club chairman, to Hitler. There was much talk of 'the callousness and heartlessness' shown to Boycott by the club. No one remotely suggested that Boycott had done anything common or mean in his entire life until, after the meeting, an old gent went up to Fielden and disarmingly said that he had known Boycott for years and that his language was disgusting. For the first time Fielden looked discomfited.

Fielden is an interesting figure. If the rebels win he could well become one of the most significant men in English cricket. Cedric Rhoades, who has been running Lancashire for so long that he has become part of the establishment, took power in very similar circumstances. Like Boycott, Fielden is no boozer. While the gin and tonic is flowing in the committee room he goes round the ground handing out newsletters and listening to members' grievances. He even holds district surgeries, a phrase he used without a trace of irony. At Goole, apparently 45 out of the 70 local members turned up. This extraordinary approach is likely to be adopted all over Yorkshire at the forthcoming elections. Boycott was sacked by 18 votes to eight. There will be a concerted attempt to unseat those of the 18 whose three-year term is up this winter.

One of the purposes of the Harrogate meeting was to introduce a man with the excellent Yorkshire name of Roy Ickeringill who is to stand against the chairman of the cricket sub-committee, Ronnie Burnet, one of Boycott's most influential opponents, in Harrogate. This is highly optimistic because (a) Harrogate is regarded as being as conservative in its cricketing views as in everything else, (b) Burnet is one of the most famous names in Yorkshire cricket, and (c) Ickeringill is not. But he intends to contact every Yorkshire member in the district before they vote. On reflection, the Labour Party has never been that efficient.

It may be that the remaining rebel rallies – starting next Sunday in Sheffield – will produce more passion than was seen in staid old Harrogate. But one was struck by the alacrity with which virtually everyone who spoke denigrated just about everyone else connected with cricket in Yorkshire, except Boycott. After two hours, it had become very boring to an agnostic. It would, however, be a brave man to bet that Boycott will not somehow play for Yorkshire next summer.[1]

---

[1] The rebels won, Boycott, Ickeringill and all, though Fielden soon became disillusioned with his hero.

ENGLAND DESERVE THE BIRD
February 1984

Christchurch: Shortly before the end came in the second Test yesterday, the seagulls that had been perched on top of the Christchurch scoreboard all through the match suddenly flew down, *en masse* and squawking, almost onto the square itself. They have a finely tuned instinct for rubbish.

The argument that will persist about this game will concern which was the more trashy: the pitch or England's performance on it. Before considering that, one has to take in the magnitude of England's defeat, a humiliation so complete that it boggles the mind. England lost by an innings and 132 runs, which is not unprecedented in Tests against Australia or the modern West Indies. But this was against New Zealand.

England were bowled out for 82 and 93. There are only five previous instances since the First World War of England's being bowled out even once in a Test match for under 100. It has not happened twice in a match this century. The two previous instances both date from the early days of organised international cricket in cases where wickets, which were probably rough and primitive in any case, were left open to storms. There was nothing wrong with the Christchurch covers.

And it all happened so quickly. England's last three-day Test was 12 years ago (the victory over Australia at Leeds in 1972). But there was no play before 4.30 this Saturday. The match finished yesterday at 4.31 precisely. Except for the one minute, it was a two-day Test. England had lost in two days in 1921 to Warwick Armstrong's brilliant Australians. This – you almost have to pinch yourself as you repeat it – was

42

against New Zealand, who until six years ago had never beaten England at all.

There is no doubt that it was a bad wicket. Bob Willis called it a disgrace and though the New Zealanders were less blunt – for on this point the embarrassment is theirs – the message was not dissimilar. Bob Vance, the chairman of the New Zealand Cricket Council, said rather sheepishly: 'It was not quite up to Test standard': he refused to comment on whether it had been right to leave the Test at Christchurch, after the only two previous games here this season finished inside two days, rather than move it to Napier. It was possible to detect some anger with the Christchurch committee men, who had assured him that the pitch would be all right.

But both teams had to play on the same pitch. It may perhaps have been a shade moist on Saturday afternoon after the rain. Willis thought it was deteriorating fast. Geoff Howarth, the New Zealand captain, thought it was actually playing a little more reliably yesterday. 'If these guys are thinking that the wicket's going to do something all the time, that's their problem, not ours.'

The two captains had analysed the situation very differently before the match. Willis concluded that it would be a waste of time playing a spin bowler and on Friday condoned – or did nothing to stop – a policy of constant short pitching. The New Zealanders decided that Steve Boock, the slow left-armer, could play an important part – and he did, especially in undermining the confidence of England's two left-handers, Fowler and Gower, as the bowlers' footmarks turned into rough outside their off-stump. New Zealand also reasoned that if they bowled a full length in the region of off-stump to all the batsmen on this pitch, they could let the ball do the work and wait for the nicks. Thirteen of the 20 England wickets fell to catches between wicket-keeper and gully, all expertly taken. The same policy won New Zealand the Headingley Test last year on a not dissimilar pitch. Here even the honest yeoman Chatfield seemed unplayable.

But it remains quite staggering that an England team, including an extra batsman against just this sort of contingency, could muster only 14 boundaries (several of those off the edge) and 175 runs in two innings lasting for just six hours. This is not a bad England batting team. Names like Gower and Botham will ring down the ages for their deeds on other occasions.

But the game of cricket is played inside the players' heads as much as it is played on a 22-yard strip, and it is in their heads that England lost this game. They had decided the situation was hopeless and so, inevitably, hopeless it became. Possibly the very presence of the extra batsman is psychologically unfortunate, making all of them think they have less responsibility. Yet Willis did not criticise them at all. All over Australia last year he marked each disaster by saying how lazy and incompetent the batsmen were, when one felt that a little self-criticism of the way he and Botham were bowling might have been appropriate. Yesterday he was scathing about the bowlers.

It was an interesting semantic exercise since apart from a halfhearted exemption of Pigott ('for a guy bowling in his first game, he did quite well early on'), he left only three people: himself, whom he appeared not to mean, Cowans, who bowled pretty well most of the time, and the man whom Willis described after the Wellington Test as the greatest advertisement for cricket that the game possessed, Botham. It would be hard to say anything that was legal, decent, honest and truthful about Botham's performance in this match. But here once again there was a difference with Howarth. He called England's batting inept.

There was not much that could be done to retrieve England's first innings yesterday. They resumed at 53 for seven, needing to get 108 to avoid the follow-on, and never looked like doing it. Gatting, who had gone in at No 7 because of a damaged shoulder, avoided getting out. The tail put up as much resistance as could reasonably be expected and England were all out, 225 runs behind, at 12.15.

Howarth did not think long before making England bat again. Fowler and Tavare walked out to face 35 minutes before lunch and at first nothing went wrong. It was a cool and cloudy day. Would England battle it out and hope that rain might return? Not a chance. Many of these batsmen have an adequate technique but dubious attitude. With Tavare, the reverse may be true. He stepped back, dangled the bat at Hadlee and was caught behind. His first-innings dismissal was very similar.

Gower, who more than anyone gave the impression that the pitch might leap up and bite him, pushed forward and was caught at fourth slip; Fowler was again out to Boock, to a ball that bounced more than he expected, which he pushed to silly point; Gatting cover-drove and thick-edged to first slip. Enter Botham, this time without his first-innings helmet. Boock flighted the first ball, Botham on-drove, got an inside edge and found Martin Crowe's left hand at forward short leg. Thirty-one for five. Exit Botham, for some reason smiling.

Randall, on a pair, avoided the hat-trick. Then Coney scooped up a catch at second slip to remove Lamb. Thirty-three for six. Then after 16 wickets came a little resistance from Randall and Taylor, two instinctive fighters. The stand was broken unluckily, Taylor slipping as he changed his mind about a single into the covers. Seventy-two for seven.

By now Hadlee was back in the attack and there was no batting to come. The clouds were too high over the hills to hope for anything from them. Even Randall could not fight on and was caught by Cairns, juggling at third slip. Willis was caught by one of the predatory gullies. Cowans had a brief slog, edged, and it was all over. There was time for Pigott, if he could uncancel the invitations, to go ahead and have his wedding today as planned. But who among this lot would you choose as best man?

HELP! I'M A STRANGER IN PARADISE
February 1984

Somewhere in the Antipodes: Following the unfortunate destruction of earth by the Vogons in *The Hitchhiker's Guide to the Galaxy*, one of the characters has the job of rebuilding it. No one said it had to be exactly the same. In case fantasy ever becomes fact it might be best to get in a few recommendations on the new version of Britain in advance.

I think we should keep it roughly the same size, but with a fraction of the population. Move it a bit nearer the Equator but nowhere too hot or dry; somewhere further away from Reagan and Chernenko (the people who might make this exercise necessary); the green of England for the most part, but a bit more spectacular – we'll throw in a few volcanos and fjords; and a few of the old things the British threw away....

But of course it all exists already, as far away from home as you can get, here in Little England beyond the world: unretouched pubs, elm trees, press Button 'A' phone boxes, chugging old Morris 1000s and Austins of England – a sentimentalised version of British life, short only of steam trains. There is even a successful cricket team, which is more than the real England has at the moment. And for the first time New Zealand has constituted the major part of an England tour. The success of the home players has justified the trip. Never again is the country likely to be considered a place that has to be visited for appearances' sake at the end of an Ashes series when everyone wants to go home.

Yet it is a strange tour, strange because everything is so familiar. The other tours take on their initial character from the nature of the land; the harsh glare of Australia, the exotic muddle of India, the vibrancy and variety of the West Indies. Here, in a very cool and damp New Zealand summer (it would be a below-average English summer too and only the thought that it is really February stops us moaning), it has at times been hard to remember that we are not spending a gloomy May pottering round the English county circuit, except that several of the places we have visited lack the urban sophistication and teeming night life of, say, Hinckley or Worksop.

The similarity has been greatest in the cricket itself. No one has to make major adjustments to cope with the pitches. They have, for the most part, been pretty poor but English cricketers are used to that. It was unfortunate that the one really good wicket was at Palmerston North, where there was a gale on all three days, making the match a misery. It could easily have happened at Nuneaton.

There are some differences for the players. The grass is a little different, though its cricketing properties are much the same; the relationship with the umpires is less chatty, more distant – Fred Goodall and Steve Woodward who did all three tests, are regarded quite highly (for foreigners) but they are not old players and do not mix much; and some men find it hard to play on grounds like Auckland and Christchurch which are primarily rugby stadiums. The dressing-rooms have no view of the play and at Auckland in particular, where the cricket is laid diagonally across the rugby pitch, it is hard for everyone to get their bearings.

But this is minimal stuff. A week on Monday we all head off for Pakistan, and we ain't seen nothing yet. It is good that New Zealand has emerged as a suitable site for a fullish tour. England needed a replacement for South Africa to keep the four-year cycle going, and they have found one with no political hang-ups. New Zealand need to improve the net wickets and some of their organisation but not half as much as England need to improve their cricket.

And yet these tiny administrative flaws seem somehow endemic. There is a curious torpor about the country. With some difficulty I have avoided the old gag about arriving in New Zealand and finding it closed, but only because it is hackneyed – not because it was untrue. There is a reason for it. In 1935 New Zealand elected a Labour government under Michael Savage, which decided to fight the depression by Rooseveltian methods. These included a five-day week for just about everyone including for instance, shop workers. Very recently, a few shops have begun opening on a Saturday morning; this is considered very daring. If you employ someone on Saturday or Sunday, you have to pay penal rates and the employee faces penal taxation. As a result, there is something awesome about a New Zealand wet weekend; it is like an English Christmas. In Auckland, there is a huge monument to Savage.

Australian weekends are fairly total too, but their society has been changed utterly by immigration from southern

47

Europe. It has become cosmopolitan; people go out, eat late, try different things. Here almost all the restaurants shut before 9.30 p.m. New Zealand provides the best example of what British people do when left on their own to create a society; the answer is their gardens. I loved the young-country excitement of Australia and was disappointed not to find it here. You feel rotten complaining to anyone about it, because all the people are friendly, the women sweet and smiling, and everyone will do everything they can to help, at least as long as it does not mean them working one minute over their allotted time.

I can well see that this *mañana* life out here among the red phone boxes, the belisha beacons, the tin roof bungalows (all traditionally with a quarter acre of land) the roses, the hydrangeas, the sparrows, the hedgehogs and the huge steaks, might well appeal to many people as an earthly paradise. There is no conflict in society, Springbok tours and one-day cricket matches sometimes excepted. Sheep may safely graze and I try to tell myself (as an infomaniac, certified and incurable) that the boringness of New Zealand's newspapers is a sign of the country's essential good health. It was good to read yesterday that there has been no problem with the new telephone directory in Timaru.

But perhaps all of us have a need for a touch of drama, a bit of pizazz. Certainly, a journalist does. 'I am glad a place like New Zealand exists,' said one of the tabloid boys on the tour, 'I just don't want to exist here.' I think I share the sentiments. Earthly paradise may be fine for other people. For myself, I prefer life.

GLORIOUS GREENIDGE MAKES ENGLAND PAY
July 1984

Four days of roughly equal cricket had lulled everyone into a false sense of security, David Gower perhaps most of all. Yesterday, after declaring and setting the West Indies a target that would look a shade generous against most county sides, Gower and England were destroyed by nine wickets.

It was obvious before play began that if Richards got in and went berserk then all England's calculations would be meaningless. We had forgotten Greenidge. He made 214 not out, the first double century ever by a West Indian in a Lord's Test. It took only five hours and Gomes stayed with him in an unbroken stand of 287. From mid-afternoon it was obvious that the West Indians were going to win. They did it with 11.5 overs to spare. Richards was not even required.

The last time England lost the first two games of a home series was against the 1948 Australians. Orwell was the first person to make the connection between 1948 and 1984, and indeed one did have the sense of a chilling superior force at work yesterday.

After the Lord's defeat against Australia England responded by dropping Hutton. If we had a Hutton now, perhaps we could drop him. Instead the selectors will again have to contemplate the deficiencies of the bowling, a point obscured by Botham's superhuman exertions on Saturday. That seemed very distant yesterday, though Godfrey Evans recalled it by breaking with precedent and naming Greenidge and Botham as joint men of the match. In his capacity as official odds-maker, Evans had sent the West Indians out to 6-1 before play began. That is even less likely to be repeated this summer than the joint award.

Gower is captain for the season, so he is fireproof in that respect. He would have saved himself from criticism had he not declared, though there were no cries of horror audible when it happened. At the time England had batted on for 20 minutes, scored 13 runs, which were neither here nor there, and lost two wickets. Foster was in with only Willis to come, so the end was almost certainly nigh anyway.

The West Indians had to score 342 in 330 minutes. The major argument against them getting it was history, both of this match – in which not even Richards had made batting look entirely easy – and before. Only four teams have scored more to win a Test match. And for the first half hour, in which only 10 runs came, a dead draw looked most probable.

At that moment, Greenidge cut loose. He never stopped. He is probably the most ferocious player in the world in the segment between gully and cover, and from an early stage Gower had positioned Fowler in a run-saving position on the Greenidge meridian. Some he stopped, most he could hardly see.

What could England have done? They could have bowled a more sensible line not, of all things, given Greenidge scope to square-cut downhill to the short boundary. Gower might have tried bowling Gatting or even Broad to vary the pace on the offchance of breaking the batsmen's concentration; they could hardly have done worse than the main bowlers.

The fielders might have held the few chances that were offered. Gomes was put down by Pringle on five and Greenidge by Botham on 110, both in the slips, though on reflection these would only have brought Richards in.

Gower might also have bowled Miller more. Next to Willis, he looked the most likely to slow the scoring-rate, and if you cannot look to your spinner to buy a wicket in these circumstances, there is no point in playing one.

One does not imagine that any of this made a difference. When Greenidge did not get room to cut, he square- or straight-drove, often savagely, or tucked the ball off his legs. Gomes, meanwhile, was his quiet but increasingly formidable self: often seeming only to nudge the over-pitched ball square, but somehow getting four past an increasingly ragged load of fielders.

The day's best bit of fielding accounted for the one wicket – Lamb hitting the stumps from square leg as Haynes scurried back too late after contemplating an impertinent single. Greenidge then so dominated matters that Gomes missed his century by eight. Greenidge even had the impertinence to reach his 200 with a six from what looked like a top-edged hook. By then, the two had broken the record second-wicket stand for the West Indies against England (previously 249); Greenidge had become only the third post-war player to make 200 in a Lord's Test (following Donnelly of New Zealand and Mohsin of Pakistan) and new, amazing statistics were rolling off the conveyor belt by the minute.

One at least was consoling for England: the Haynes wicket was the first second-innings one the West Indies have lost in the last eight Tests. They have now won five running, since the middle of their home series against Australia in the spring: by 10 wickets, an innings and 36, 10 wickets, an innings and 180 and now nine wickets.

Gower denied a suggestion that he was watching television when Lamb and Pringle might have been given guidance about staying on the field on Monday night, but admitted it might have been better had he been on the balcony. Perhaps, if England are to have any chance of winning a game this series, Gower might have to adopt a slightly less laid-back style of leadership. But this is not really an occasion for self-flagellation. England were beaten by a great innings at the end of a great Test match, in which receipts reached £½ million for the first time. It has been an occasion to savour.

NOTTINGHAMSHIRE LOSE THE AUTUMN GOLD

September 1984

At 6.15 on a sunlit Taunton evening – 15 minutes after the season would have ended in the days when close of play meant what it said and almost five months after it began – Essex became County champions for the second year running. One-day cricket has debased the currency, both of great finishes and of adjectives to describe them, but it would be hard for any form of the game, or any other game, to surpass the ending of the dear old County championship last night.

Nottinghamshire needed 297 to beat Somerset and thus overtake Essex. Having virtually given up hope when their captain Clive Rice was out after scoring a masterful 98, they started the final over 14 runs short with the last pair at the crease: Mike Bore, an old-fashioned tail-ender of advancing years and girth hauled out of semi-retirement as second team

51

captain because of injuries, and the tyro seam bowler Andy Pick. Facing the 20-year-old slow left-armer Steve Booth, Bore smashed the first ball to the long-on boundary first bounce, struck the second for another four through extra cover and then turned the third for a cunning two past square leg.

Four to win, three balls left. Bore, the improbable man of destiny, went on a nervous Tavare-like walkabout; Rice, in the dressing-room, could no longer bear to watch; Keith Fletcher, listening on his car radio on the ground at Chelmsford was both panic-stricken and helpless. The next ball Bore blocked. The fifth he leapt at, smashing it high and straight, but just a fraction too short. It came down into the safe hands of Somerset's substitute, a young man from Keynsham (spelt K-E-Y-N-S-H-A-M) called Richard Ollis. He can have the freedom of Chelmsford if he wants it.

The match was over, won by Somerset by three runs. The title, pennant, trophy and £15,000 booty from Britannic Assurance's first year of sponsorship thus went to Fletcher and Essex, the first team ever to do the championship/Sunday League double and the first to retain the championship since Yorkshire in 1968. The winners' cheque that had been written out for Nottinghamshire had to be torn up, though they got £7,500 as runners-up and Hadlee won a new award, worth £500 for player of the year. Middlesex were third and Leicestershire fourth. It has to be said that the better and best team won.

The extraordinary finale was set up by an excellent declaration from Ian Botham. His obligation was to set the target that would give his team their best chance of winning, though whether Somerset finished eighth or ninth was probably not the weightiest matter on his mind. He judged it just right: 297 in a minimum of 52 overs, or just over three hours, since the pitch was turning and Marks and Booth were able to bowl above the union rate. It was not especially generous, but the short Taunton boundaries still encourage the adventurous batsman as they did when Wellard and Gimblett were going. Broad, not normally in that class as a hitter, hit 12 off Crowe's second over, and the race was on.

Broad dominated the opening stand with Robinson. A couple of catches went down but he batted very shrewdly, using his feet to the spinners this time, and his innings might yet constitute a late hint to the England selectors, though the Newmarket whisper is that Kim Barnett of Derbyshire is now the hot fancy as an opener.[1] The first wicket made 69, but both Broad and Robinson got out just before tea. Randall drove a catch back to Marks and young Johnson was easily stumped. The big two were now together.

Hadlee, who had not bowled before the declaration, was not quite at his clean-hitting best. Rice, however, was magnificent. He rarely makes the scores he did three years ago now, favouring the handsome 40 over the big hundred, but yesterday there was a glint in his eye. It says a lot for the bowling, particularly for Booth, who looked both talented and astute, that Rice did not tear it apart, but Nottinghamshire were still making good progress; 138 were wanted when the compulsory last 20 overs began and Hadlee was just starting to middle it. Then he chipped to the mid-wicket boundary, Lloyd was there and took the catch falling onto the advertising boards.

There was some controversy about this and the vaguest hint of a riot, meaning – this being the County championship – that the three itinerant Nottinghamshire supporters in the River Stand got very agitated. However, as everyone knows without looking it up, Law 32, paragraph two, sub-section (a) clause II says that where there are boards rather than a rope, this constitutes a fair catch, and Hadlee was on his way.

Still Rice was going well; 84 were wanted off 12 and, after an incredible flat six over extra cover, 56 off seven. Then he holed out to Ollis at deep square. Surely it was over now. Cooper and Hemmings charged and were easily stumped. Essex began to relax, but everyone had reckoned without Bore. Twenty-seven were needed off two overs and a simple pick-up six off Marks set up the conclusion.

There have been superb finishes to the championship before – 1977, for instance, when Gloucestershire chucked it away on the last day and 1959 when Yorkshire made a near-impossible target at Hove – but probably nothing like this. It says something for the nature of the competition that it should be settled in the end by the conjunction, not of the big names, but of Bore, Booth and Ollis, and that the eventual champions were Essex, who by their all-round strength – their overseas stars fitting into the pattern, not dominating it – entirely deserved it.

[1] Wrong.

A PAUSE FOR CHEERFUL THOUGHT
September 1984

Suddenly everything is mellow and the 1984 cricket season is already starting to recede from the sports pages and towards next year's Wisden and our memories, where it will be forever remembered with the warm, sepia glow that attends past dry and memorable summers.

Keith Fletcher has it all now, or almost all; the Cawdor and Glamis of championship and Sunday League cannot compensate for the fact that he will never be king hereafter, not while Peter May is running the show. And in a sense the anomaly of Fletcher's position – undisputed monarch of the county game, untouchable at international level – illustrates better than anything else the strange divide in professional cricket.

Most people will remember 1984 for the sight of English cricketers darting out of the way of West Indian bouncers, with varying degrees of success, and then making charlies of themselves against Sri Lanka. The *Guardian* leader-writer used the word 'nadir' and quite right too. At least I hope it is right; I can't bear to think what the next depth might be.

And yet, on a different level, an entirely contrasting story emerged. The 1984 season produced 326 first class centuries, a figure surpassed only twice since the war – in 1947 and 1959, when more first class matches were played. To an extent this might be put down to the dry weather and a certain reflation of the fixture list – Nottinghamshire, for instance, played 28 three-day matches, a figure that takes them back almost to the levels prior to the invention of the one-day game.

But there are other indicators. Perhaps the most telling statistic is that only three bowlers – Hadlee, Allott and Underwood – averaged under 20. In the 1950s and 1960s, it was not uncommon for 30 and 40 players to beat this figure. If anyone has the patience to work it out, they could almost certainly prove that the average of runs per wicket was higher in English cricket this year than at any time in the past. In other words, the bat is wholly dominating the ball.

These runs are not being scored by foreigners either. The slow squeeze on overseas recruitment, plus the absence of Richards, Greenidge and Lloyd on tour, meant that only two foreign players, Kallicharran and McEwan, played full-time in county cricket just for their batting this year, though there were still plenty of overseas bowlers. And the runs were not coming from old men.

In the 1970s, if an Englishman aged 21 or under scored a championship hundred, half the sages would plonk him in their England team on the spot. In the case of Gooch, the selectors did, with, at that time, disastrous results. Now a player like Ian Butcher of Leicestershire can score five centuries and not a dog barks.

The immediate reaction of the Bedser/Trueman school of thought, which holds that cricket worth talking about ceased 20 years ago, is that no one can bowl any more. We shall examine this possibility in a moment. But, on the figures, the best generation of English batsmen for many, many years is emerging, the majority playing with a new method of which Gooch was the forerunner: premature backlift, heavy bat, upright stance, wallop. Robert Bailey was desperately close to the tour this winter; some of this generation are certain to play for England inside two years.

Until they are picked, we may never find out how good they are. They need to be tested, but whether or not the bowlers in county cricket are good enough to do it, conditions at present are weighted against them. The pitches are uneven, but mostly so turgid that these gum-chewing young bucks have heaps of time to decide whether they are going to despatch the ball off their toes or their knees. It may well be that the soils of many county grounds are too played out, after 100 years or longer, to provide decent wickets. Under the circumstances, the odd bit of, er, shall we say, creative groundsmanship, that goes on in certain places comes as a relief. As long as they do not overdo it, a Trent Bridge greentop provides an infinitely more appealing match than a muckheap, where you know in advance that the first two and a half days are simply the prelude to the target cricket of the fourth innings.

The answer does not lie in four-day cricket. The county game still has some vitality; that way would be lingering death. What the counties should do is restore some of the old variety, the old uncertainty, by leaving wickets uncovered. When full covering was brought in four years ago, it was said that, to compensate spin bowlers, groundsmen would be asked to prepare dry pitches. The result has been wickets that are too slow to compensate anyone, not least the spectator. On a sticky dog at Hastings or Folkestone, with Underwood making the ball rear throatwards, we might find out just how good this new generation is. We might also unearth a new Underwood.[1]

Pessimism about English cricket is part of our heritage, and we need it most of all in warm summers like this one. Otherwise, we would have to be happy which would be unbearable. But it might be best not to overdo the gloom. The game is richer and healthier than anyone could have imagined a few years ago, when it seemed destined for gentle decline towards the museum, like the nation itself. Given young bowlers to match the young batsmen, it is not impossible that the national team may soon begin to reassert itself. From the nadir might yet come a new golden age.

---

[1] Uncovered pitches were tried again, in 1987, then quickly scrapped.

SUBJECT: ENGLAND'S FAILINGS
December 1984

Delhi: Memo to the working party charged with discovering why England, after 13 Test matches this year, have failed to win any of them, and currently look unlikely to win the 14th. A less-than-exhaustive list of reasons, ranging from the general to the particular:

1   The bias against excellence throughout British society, which makes extreme determination to succeed in sport almost inseparable from dottiness.

2   The near-collapse of organised cricket through much of the state school system, only partly compensated for by the growth of clubs.

3   The improvement of standards elsewhere in the world, helped by English professional coaching, the opportunities provided to foreign players by English counties, better facilities (in most cases), a more competitive atmosphere and a more favourable climate.

4   The weakness of the early-to-mid 1970s intake into the English counties, and the consequent absence of players who should now be at their peak. The next generation should be better, partly due to Packerism (more money in cricket) and Thatcherism (fewer alternatives).

5   The ban on the players who went to South Africa.

6   Slow, covered English wickets, which work against the development of the most important cricketing skills: good fast bowling, good spin bowling, attacking but technically sound stroke-play.

7   The role of the Sunday League, which does ditto, and even more so.

8   An overloaded international fixture list, which creates staleness and a sense of drudgery.

9   Unimaginative captaincy.

10   Garner.

11   Marshall.

12   Holding.

13   Inconsistent and ill-informed selection policies, made by men who do not see any cricket on tours and insufficient

county cricket to acquire accurate information. This results particularly in the selection of the right players at the wrong time or for the wrong job (Randall, Pigott, Nick Cook, for example).

14 The fact that when a working party is set up, it includes several people (not least the chairman of selectors) who might be presumed responsible for at least some of the above. It hardly suggests a fresh approach.

HAIL OF ORANGES IS INDIA'S JUST DESSERT
January 1985

Calcutta: The cricket here yesterday veered away from the predictably dull and at times lurched towards the disgraceful. The match is dead. But one of the joys of the game is that even in the most turgid match there can be absolutely fascinating sub-plots. Yesterday there were three riveting little contests: David Gower fighting the demon of bad form (he lost again, I'm afraid); Sivarama's leg-spin against England's batsmen in general (still in progress); and Sunil Gavaskar against what now appears to be the rest of India, if not the world.

Gavaskar's tactics as Indian captain yesterday were utterly bewildering. He allowed the Indian innings to drone on until 20 minutes after lunch – and this, remember, was the fourth day – to no purpose whatever. India's very slender chance of converting this drawn match into a victory rested on hitting a few quick runs after yesterday's crawl and then whipping England out twice. India excluded that option. In the two hours before lunch, they scored only 69 runs and lost two more wickets. By the close, England were 99 for two in reply to 437 for seven declared. It is a ludicrous situation. One should, I think, be rather encouraged that the crowd see it that way too.

When India still went on after lunch, they chanted the local

58

equivalent of 'Gavaskar out' and made ineffectual attempts to throw fruit at the Indian dressing-room. One tomato winged this correspondent, who was innocent. When the declaration came, after more than 13 hours' batting, the day's orange peel was thrown onto the pitch and there was a further 10-minute delay while it was cleared up by three men with one bucket. A kitehawk even caught the spirit of the day by dropping a loaf of bread from its talons where mid-on might have been.

When Gavaskar was obliged to chase towards the boundary and again at the close, there were further lashings of orange peel in his direction. The 1,300 police were reinforced to ensure the Indians' safety. But, I think on the whole, the spectators may be behaving more sensibly than the captain.

Later Gavaskar said he would never play in Calcutta again because of the crowd's abuse. He said they had not understood his policy, which was to score 450 and put England under pressure. 'It was the only route to a positive result.' Fair enough, but the runs had to be made with some urgency. As it was, no one understood his policy, because it was incomprehensible. On this basis, he might have to play all his future cricket in private.

On Thursday, everyone had sat with remarkable stoicism through the batting of Azharuddin and Shastri, who has enough experience to have done better. One began to think this was an oriental version of Yorkshire, whose supporters seem able to appreciate Boycott's feats without any regard to their context. Yesterday, fewer people turned up – a mere 60,000 or so – and they were decidedly less stoical. Shastri, meanwhile, condemned himself: 'Nothing was going to come in the way of my getting a century,' he told the local paper. Well, thanks a bunch, mate. Never mind the spectators, or the poor suffering game; just as long as you get your century.

He batted for seven and a half hours for his 111 before Cowans ducked one into his off-stump. What happened later was no better. Kirmani made some effort to force the pace; Prabhakar, who can hit the ball hard, made no attempt to do so. Never were India in more need of Kapil Dev. After lunch, Gower bowled himself, which was one comment. The batsmen treated him seriously, which was another.

But there was still some cricket to be seen, important for the series if not for this match. England went in needing 238 to avoid the follow-on. The openers saw off the new ball all right, but then Robinson had to go off because some grit had worked its way behind his contact lens. (A worrying one for the scorers, that. He was not really retired hurt or retired ill, nor was he emulating the famous scorebook entries of the past, absent bathing, and absent dead – retired unsighted, perhaps.) That brought in Gower, who had moved himself back up the order to try to sort out his own problems which, in a quieter way, are as pressing as Gavaskar's. Gower needs runs.

Soon after his arrival, Gower played his best shot for weeks, a square flick for four off Chetan Sharma. But Sivarama was on now and though he could not extract any bounce from this wicket, his wrist action was enough to get turn. Five balls in a row, three just before tea, two just after, had Gower in trouble. One of these was yet another pad and alleged bat catch to Vengsarkar at silly point, which umpire Raju ruled not out. Vengsarkar was livid, and Gower began arguing with Gavaskar at slip about the amount of lip going on. They went into tea shaking hands, and the captains agreed they were still friends. As one of the England players remarked, Gower may be the last Gavaskar has. But Gower found Sivarama far from friendly. Finally, desperation crept in against Yadav, he drove expansively and was caught at cover for 19. His last seven innings have brought 70 runs. There will be no tiger hunts for him when England are playing South Zone next week.

Fowler, meanwhile, was playing patchily, troubled sometimes by the low bounce, occasionally thumping the leg-break, turning into the left-hander over mid-wicket. When he was on 49, that ploy failed and he was caught there, Sivarama's 20th victim of the series. Pocock endured the last over. The mandatory 80 were not finished, for the first time – but the light had gone.

There was one other little test of nerve, which was undoubtedly won by Bruce French, England's reserve wicket-keeper and rock climber. Having returned from his side trip to Katmandu, he went onto the mountain-high roof of the stand to take a picture, dangling his feet over the edge to the horror of the constabulary. One of their 1,300 was despatched, shaking. By the time he had reached the roof French, picture taken, was happily on his way down.

GATTING AND FOWLER DOUBLE UP INDIANS
January 1985

Madras: The England innings yesterday assumed Himalayan proportions, comparable with the greatest performances in the history of English batsmanship. England and India go into the rest day of the fourth Test amid the debris of English batting records and Indian broken hearts. Above it all stand Mike Gatting and Graeme Fowler, both of whom began this series with their quality as Test players in doubt, and who have now become the first England batsmen in 108 years and 610 matches to score double centuries in the same Test innings.

With two days of the Test remaining England are, astonishingly, 611 for five, 339 ahead of India. The only worries one has are whether any of this will prevent the game being any less drawn than the one in Calcutta and whether one might not wake up with a screaming hangover and discover we are really back in Christchurch.

The bare figures are suffocating. Fowler scored 201, which was a record for any Englishman in a Test in India and stood for around three hours until Gatting passed him on the way to 207. The total was not only England's highest in India but their highest in any overseas Test since the Second World War and the timeless Test at Durban in 1938-39, which went on almost as long. The interim scores will be statistical benchmarks for years to come. England were 563 for two before Lamb was out. Even in Hutton's Test at The Oval in 1938, the third wicket fell at 546. The highest score at which England have ever lost their second wicket was 425 at

61

Melbourne in 1911-12. Fowler was second out just six runs short of that.

For two days, everything has gone right for English cricket. But will it mean anything come Friday night? The wicket is now playing extremely easily, except for the first faint traces of bowlers' rough. The local theory is that the heavy rain which fell on Madras last week will bind the wicket a good deal better than the usual salty water poured on when the pitch is being prepared. Batting may be just as straightforward 48 hours hence as Fowler and Gatting have made it look.

Much is bound to depend on the Indians' state of mind, after they have had the rest day to recover. Ideally, England ought to have whizzed the Indians in for a few overs from a fresh Cowans and Foster last night when their demoralisation was still fresh. Now England may well bat on briefly tomorrow morning after getting the heavy roller on to try and hasten the ravages of time. The 654 of Durban may yet be surpassed. Had India gone in again, Gavaskar would have been able to bat. He was off the field from lunchtime onwards, after an allergy made his hands swell and go green. Most fielding captains are allergic to 611 for five.

The first three partnerships of the England innings were worth 178 (Fowler and Robinson on Monday), 241 (Fowler and Gatting) and 144 (Gatting and Lamb). After that, Edmonds and Foster were sent in to slog. Only once before have the first two England wickets put on 150 each – against India at Edgbaston in 1974. This match was particularly relevant: David Lloyd, Fowler's fellow-Accringtonian, scored 214 not out, and the one figure Fowler really wanted to beat, for purposes of lighthearted banter until old age, was that one.

He has nothing else to feel sorry about. Oh, he still played and missed outside off-stump on rare occasions, but the strength of his run-getting was on the off-side between square and extra cover. He resisted his habit of lofting the off-spinner over mid-on until he was past 180 when he smashed two sixes off Yadav in the same over, removing him from the attack and conceivably from the Indian team.

He did not give another chance (there was nothing

clear-cut all day until Foster was put down at long-on) and, apparently, gave one less than one had thought on Monday. Fowler says he did not nick the ball early on when Kirmani dived and missed, and was undoubtedly telling the truth. He has never been afraid to admit his failings. Other people have often been afraid to give him full credit for his skill and character. Whether or not the return of Gooch and the rest knocks him out of the Test team, he will be a force in English cricket for years to come.

But in the end he was overshadowed. Gavaskar described Gatting's innings as magnificent, and there is no point looking for another word. In the morning, when the Indians bowled more tightly than at any stage of the match, he was content to wait. Only 75 runs came in the session, the quietest period of an unquiet match. With Gatting, though, you know that if the ball is there to be hit, he will hit it. He built his innings with the utmost care, reached his century in five hours – it was after tea that he set out to do what he can do as effectively as any other contemporary English batsmen, Gooch included, which is trample on an already broken attack.

Having waited 31 Tests for his first 100, the 200 target three Tests later never bothered him – twice in the 190s he reverse swept Shastri and when he reached 200 the spectators applauded him as generously as they would have done the local boy Srikkanth. The crowd indeed was most appreciative throughout – they warmly applauded Lamb when he reached 50. They enjoyed the Sunday stuff at the end when England concentrated on quick runs.

Gatting holed out at long-on. Gower, who was originally padded up to go in No 3, held back to let Edmonds and Foster go in and slog. Lamb and Foster got out swiping the inswingers of Amarnath, the acting captain who brought himself on after 145 overs when all the other options had failed. Gower eventually arrived at No 7. It would have been nice had he joined in more, but he is presiding over the resurrection of English cricket's self-respect, and that is something of which we can all be proud.

CAPTAIN GOWER RISES TO THE ASHES
September 1985

The end came with extraordinary rapidity. Australia were 129 all out, losing their last six wickets in only 95 minutes yesterday, and before even getting a chance to unpack their picnics, the crowd were filing across The Oval outfield to hear the speeches or, rather, this being 1985, the television interviews. England had won the final Test by an innings and 94, the first time since 1956 they have beaten Australia by an innings twice running. The Ashes are back by three Tests to one and England have won three successive home series against Australia for the first time since W. G.'s day in the 1890s.

The packed house gave the occasion a flavour it would have lost had Australia resisted into Tuesday. But the spectators were as good as gold. Only three youths attempted the old trick of dashing on as the final wicket fell. Everyone else filed stoically towards the pavilion in the Great British queuing tradition. David Gower then appeared on the balcony and gave a Princess Di wave, half-regal, half-shy. The interviewer, Peter West, mentioned The Oval's most famous balcony-crowd scene, 1953, when England, under Hutton, won the Ashes for the first time since the war. Gower looked blank and said he wasn't born then. But later, in the quiet of the Surrey Library with W. G. staring down at him, Gower had enough sense of history to say it was the greatest moment of his career. He was also man of the series for his 732 runs (Gooch was man of this particular match).

Border's first answer to West was drowned in the applause from the throng: recognition for a very worthy opponent indeed. Gower thought that summed up the amity of the series, which it did, as did the sneak pictures in yesterday's papers. Border, late on Saturday in Mayfair, was accompanied not by the traditional Mayfair sort of companion but by Botham. The 1985 Australians have delighted everyone with their affability towards the opponents and their please-and-thank-you to everyone. Alas, not with their cricket, though. Border yesterday would not even argue with the idea that the Australians were the weakest ever.

Gower thought the balance of England's attack, in the last couple of Tests, had been a great asset. This included Botham operating as a genuine quick bowler, which again is not something that could have been easily predicted on recent form. He also noted the batsmen's new habit of making big centuries. There were eight England hundreds in the series, but no Englishman was out anywhere between 86 and 148.

The last phase of the series yesterday belonged primarily to the Lion of Edgbaston, Richard Ellison, who finished with five for 46 to give him 17 in the past two Tests. But the Australians might have got out to anyone yesterday.

The management was annoyed at the start, following reports that they had refused to play in the hypothetical beer match if the Test finished early. The TCCB were offering £10,000 prize money, twice as much as England got for winning the real game, and it was Gower who rejected the idea.

Some thought the Australians played at the end as though they were in a beer match already: Ritchie was caught behind, driving; the Phillips square-cut, which has given England more wickets than the Hilditch hook (though it has given him plenty of runs too), brought Botham his 31st victim of the series. Then Border, who has spent the summer like Horatius on the bridge while Lars Porsena Botham scared off everyone else, edged a slanting Ellison delivery to second slip, and England were through.

The last three wickets fell in two overs. Lawson drove at a wide one, Botham took a cat-like slip catch to dismiss McDermott. It was so dark that Bennett removed his customary sunglasses before giving Taylor the soft return catch that settled the match (an hour later it was raining hard). Even without Bennett's specs, the field now was full of shades – of 1953 and 1926, of Hutton and Percy Chapman, the only other England captains to recapture the Ashes here. Despite all the weaknesses, many of the performances in this series are fit to rank in the pantheon: the batting of Border, Ritchie, Gooch, Robinson, Gatting and, above all, Gower; the bowling of McDermott and Botham.

For Gower, even greater glory beckons. For once, England

have a long holiday. Their next Test, in Kingston, is on 21 February. That will be the first of 15 Tests in 1986, and the players will probably not have a break longer than a month until 1988. By then, if they can take the pace, England might just be established as the world's leading cricketing nation. Gower joked yesterday about the West Indies 'quaking in their boots' but with Garner and Holding on the far side of the mountain-top and the always-fragile cohesion of the West Indians in doubt after Lloyd's retirement, there is just a chance it is not such a joke.

For now, though, England are just delighted with their achievement. And rightly so. There has been, to nick the title of Mike Brearley's account of the 1981 series, a phoenix from the Ashes too: it is David Gower.

MARSHALL RAISES THE WIND IN JAMAICA
February 1986

Kingston: All the screaming 3 a.m. horrors came true for England at Sabina Park yesterday as the West Indies' fast bowlers took a grip on the English batting they have no intention of relinquishing. West Indies won the first of the four one-day internationals by six wickets, but worse, far worse, came when Mike Gatting had his nose broken by Malcolm Marshall.

Gatting, up to now England's best batsman by far on the tour, misses the first Test on Friday for which Botham, who was forced out of yesterday's match by his groin injury, is by no means a certainty. England are starting to run out of fit and flourishing batsmen: the game began with Robinson and Gower (27 runs in five innings) both being demolished for fourth-ball noughts in Patrick Patterson's first two overs in major cricket.

The old, familiar cloud of gloom has descended over English cricket, and yesterday's defeat, England's eighth in their last nine one-day games, is merely part of the picture.

The game was one-sided from the 10th ball: Robinson was beaten by a very fast, very full and very straight delivery from Patterson. Gower, glory departed, was tempting a desperate man's foot-rooted drive when he was caught at first slip.

Gatting was different. All tour he has played with more confidence than anyone bar Botham and more skill than anyone bar none, and he alone took on this staggering array of fast bowlers as though he did not know the meaning of the word unplayable. He was attempting an authentic and aggressive hook when he missed, the ball slammed into his nose and the lights went out. They led him away blood streaming, and Gatting may not even have known that the ball had gone on to break his off-bail as well. His nose was so badly damaged that it will have to be totally reset when the swelling has gone down, and even a man of Gatting's courage cannot bank on an early return. For the moment, England have ruled out the idea of a replacement. That may not last.

The innings did recover a little through Willey and Lamb, but England made only 145 for eight in their 46 overs. It was supposed to be a 50-over match with three hours 20 mins allowed for each innings. But there is no penalty for a slow over-rate on this tour – the custom of the country, you understand. Excessive use of the bouncer is a local custom, too. But you cannot accuse the West Indians of that yesterday. The rule calling a head-high ball was invoked only four times, and had Gatting been more frightened he would not have been hit. The bowlers did pitch short – Gooch, England's top scorer, spent almost his entire innings on the back foot – but really they just bowled too fast, too well, too relentlessly.

The difference between the two sides was made clear when England unleashed Thomas, like Patterson a newcomer at this level, and Greenidge began square-cutting and straight-driving, as though fast bowlers were there for the batsman's benefit. The only reminder that cricket could be any different was Gatting, nose bandaged, countenance rueful, outside the England dressing-room.

But the worst did not quite come to the worst as far as the match itself was concerned. For one thing, West Indies began to miss catches. Richard put down a slip chance against Gooch, aggravated an old hand injury, and since there was no necessity, did not bat. I doubt if there is much chance of him missing the Test. Lamb was also put down twice in the deep, as West Indies functioned for a while under the control of Garner and auto pilot. And Lamb and Willey remained together for an hour, with Willey counter-attacking daringly.

West Indies found the target, barely three an hour, so simple that I think they got bored. A 10-wicket win looked possible until both openers were out with the score in the 80s and Richardson, supposedly out of form, began to stroke the ball with the assurance of a world beater. Towards the end, both Richardson and Gomes got out and only 13 balls were left when the winning runs came. But the gap was far greater. The line of West Indian greats seems unending and Patterson, all beefcake and biceps, looks the authentic fast bowling article.

PRESS GANG RUFFLE WELL-GROOMED GEOFFREY
February 1986

Spanish Town, Jamaica: There is a certain ramshackle tradition about Press matches on cricket tours; the borrowed kit, the carefree atmosphere, the self-deprecating remarks made even by those who really can play. No one seems to have mentioned any of this to the tyro journalist who has just joined us. He simply did not look right. The trousers fitted a little too well, the bat and pads had clearly not come out of the battered old bag containing everyone else's gear, and where in Jamaica, for heaven's sake, could he possibly have acquired a Yorkshire cap? Make no mistake G. Boycott, of the *Mail on Sunday*, packs his case a little differently from the rest of us.

But he had a point: this was a slightly better class of Press match than usual. The English and West Indian journalists had combined and taken on board three Test players:

Boycott and two former West Indies all-rounders, Maurice Foster, now a radio commentator, and Peter Lashley, the PR man for the Test match sponsors, Cable & Wireless. *The Guardian* had quickly decided that this was not an occasion to make a prat of oneself bowling donkey-drops. The opposition was the league side from the Jamaican Guinness brewery, who faced us on their own pitch at Spanish Town, which is a bit like Abbeydale in a heatwave.

Tony Becca of the *Daily Gleaner*, the Press captain, had decided his team was strong enough to have Boycott at No 3. Boycott took this rather well – 'captain's decision', he said blandly – and, anyway, he was in by the seventh over facing one Dawkins, who was just the sort of Jamaican fast bowler you get in a 35-over Wednesday nighter at home against Mount Pleasant Sorting Office II: balding, chubby but just a bit too sharp for most tastes. He was meat and drink to Geoffrey, though. This was only a 35-over match, too, but I don't suppose anyone had told him that. He batted the way he always bats. In 14 overs the man with more centuries than anyone else alive nudged and steered 32. There were two fours, though I cannot recall them offhand.

But the Press were just behind what seemed a reasonable run-rate when the second opener was out and Lashley came in. We had joked with him about running Boycott out, but no one believed he would really have the nerve. And then it happened – a quick single, yes, no, Boycott scampering back, out by a yard. Lashley doubled up with laughter, as did the rest of us, though I thought a couple of the package-tour types who came along to this in the unfortunate absence of the cricket they had paid to watch[1] looked a bit disgruntled. Geoffrey took it with reasonable good grace.

Later, when Lashley was also out, Boycott lapsed into patois: 'A good job tha' didn't do it in Yorkshire. Tha'd have needed three bobbies to get home.' Lashley tried to mollify him by mentioning that it was not the first time he had got the great man out. The previous occasion was Leeds, 1966: difficult light, Hall and Griffith out of the attack, Lashley on with his little outswingers, a hint of an edge, a low catch to Jackie Hendriks. That is Lashley's recollection, and he ought to remember – it was his only Test-match wicket. 'I don't want to talk about it,' said Geoffrey. 'It was the worst ball I ever received in Test cricket.'

[1] England had lost the Test in three days.

BOYCOTT AND ENGEL UMPIRED OUT
February 1986

Port of Spain: The cricketer Geoff Boycott was released last night after spending 18 hours under close arrest in a Port of Spain hotel after he arrived at Trinidad airport without a valid work permit. I was on the same plane from Jamaica, received the same treatment and found myself more than normally involved in this latest – and decidedly surrealistic – tie up between politics and cricket. Both of us were served with deportation orders and told to get on the first plane to London. But, since this did not leave until tonight, our passports were confiscated and we were placed under guard in adjoining rooms at the Holiday Inn.

After talks yesterday between the British High Commissioner Sir Martin Berthoud and Trinidad's External Affairs Minister Errol Mahabir, the government agreed to issue work permits to both Boycott and myself and to ensure that the 15 journalists travelling with the team would also be allowed in. They were due to arrive at about 3 a.m. London time.

However, a fee of at least £35 and possibly £120 was being demanded for each journalist; Trinidad has severe economic problems. Work permit regulations have previously been waived for journalists covering cricket tours. The decision to enforce them stringently now appears to be the first formal manifestation of the anti-tour feeling that has been simmering in Trinidad for months. It is understood that separate arrangements have been made for the players.

The Prime Minister, Mr George Chambers, has said the tour can go ahead, but that he would refuse to attend the games as his protest against the inclusion of four former

South African rebels. Boycott, who was prominently involved in the original rebel tour four years ago, has been singled out for special attack by some anti-apartheid campaigners. Mr Chambers faces a tricky election shortly and has been doing a complicated balancing act between the rising anti-South African sentiment on one hand and the vast numbers of people who want to watch cricket on the other. The two contending forces were visible even as the bizarre official ritual was enacted at the airport.

Boycott and myself had booked on the same flight, unknown to each other. Boycott, who has been engaged to provide ghosted comment pieces for the *Mail on Sunday*, has been trying all along to remain apart from the team so as not to cause any trouble. I decided to go early to investigate the situation in Trinidad.

On arrival we both received the same response from separate immigration officers, were kept at the airport for two hours while being shuffled from official to official and driven with a security man to a hotel. The officials themselves were at odds about whether to be bureaucratically off-hand with Boycott or starstruck. While one customs man attempted to separate Boycott from his precious cricket bag (unsuccessfully – Boycs would have died first) another was holding an animated conversation with Boycott: 'Do you play cricket?' Customs man: 'Oh yes. You are my hero (pause) I don't care what they say.'

An airport security officer quizzed Boycott about the virtues of current England batsmen: 'What about Wilf Slack?' 'A good county player,' said Boycott sagely, while another, po-faced, led us down endless corridors. On the journey to the hotel, by which time Boycott was getting rather tired, the driver fired cricketing questions at him to the increasing irritation of the guard. The guard woke me in the small hours to insist that I move into the room next to Boycott. He remained outside all night, refusing offers of food and drink, to give his name or to say whether he was armed or not. I think he was the most terrified participant in the saga. His replacement was much more cheerful and insisted on having my autograph to go alongside 'Best wishes, G. Boycott.'

At no point was South Africa mentioned or any indication given that the action might be personal, though Boycott believes he may have a South African stamp in his passport. 'I like Trinidad,' Boycott said. 'I've helped to win two Test matches here and I've always found the people extremely friendly. No one had ever said anything to me about work permits. I think because of my quality as a player I attract the headlines: I never sought any of this or any of the trouble at Yorkshire. I came here to do a newspaper job and just provide some of my experience as a player. I've tried very hard to stay in different hotels and not embarrass the team in any way.'

There have been widespread calls for peaceful demonstration against the tour in Trinidad, and on Tuesday there was a torchlight rally at which the Minister of Works, Maintenance and Drainage added glamour to the proceedings. His defence of Prime Minister Chambers' equivocal position was drowned out by chants of 'If Chambers supporting we, ban Gooch and Emburey.'

There are elements urging stronger action. Cecil Paul of the Committee in Defence of West Indies Cricket said people should 'strike a blow against apartheid and run the friends and companions of apartheid from Trinidad and Tobago.' I don't think I recognise that as a description of myself; but if they do mean me, I hope the nice security guard is on duty at the time.

LONG NIGHT OF THE UNOFFICIAL KNIGHT
March 1986

Port of Spain: As I understand it, everyone is entitled to be famous for 15 minutes; but if you get involved with Geoffrey Boycott, even to the extent of travelling on the same plane as him, you get an extended run. It was 23 hours before the Trinidad authorities decided I was a fit and proper person to walk around unguarded and without a deportation order, and 36 hours between the first hint of trouble and the last flicker of interest from the BBC ('Just a short Q and A, old boy, usual sort of thing ...').

Now, with normal obscurity being resumed as soon as everyone forgets the horrible snarling pic of me on the front page of one of the Trinidad morning papers, it might be possible to put the treatment of Boycott and myself into some kind of perspective. The real reason why, after years of laxity that continued until 48 hours before our arrival, Trinidad should suddenly remember its work permit rules for journalists, was still unexplained yesterday. The immigration officials would have to be unexpectedly clued up to know that I had written about South Africa; it could all have been a gigantic pro-boycott, anti-Boycott plot into which this innocent was swept, but that does not quite square with the sequence of events – we were banned from entering by different officials almost simultaneously.

It seems more probable that some kind of instruction had gone out, designed to screw up the tour in general. The team were fireproof; high-powered arrangements had been made to ensure that they would be whisked to their hotel without seeing an immigration officer or, at the airport anyway, a demonstrator. The journalists were not. Those who arrived early yesterday with the team were granted entry for only three days at first and were forced to sort out their affairs later after paying the government £120, thought to be a Test match and first class extortion record for a work permit.

The team did not get off that lightly either. The travel arrangements for this game were horrific anyway, with a scheduled arrival at 10 p.m. after a seven-hour flight, 12 hours before the start of play. Thanks to a bomb-scare in Barbados – unconnected with cricket, for once – they were three hours late and so it was 2 a.m. before they reached their hotel to get a brief kip before the full horn-blaring police escort to the ground past the next batch of demonstrators.

But after these first hints that England's matches in Trinidad were not going to be quite normal – whatever, after 10 years of intermittent political crises in cricket, normality might be – there were still two theories about what would happen next. Lyle Townsend, leader of the main anti-tour faction, was promising that his group's activities would be non-violent, creative and effective. He said there were ways to prevent something from starting that did not violate anyone's rights. Hmmmm. As the world passed through my guarded hotel room, the overwhelming impression at the eye of the hurricane was of a nation more interested in the cricket than in this tour's tangential connection with South Africa. Trinidadians still kept apologising on behalf of their country.

The British High Commission were magnificent to the potential deportees (unlike the West Indies Cricket Board, whose local representative Lance Murray, refused to help). One newspaper claimed that Sir Geoffrey Howe had intervened, but I reckon only one Sir Geoffrey was involved in this episode. And by the time we were driven back to the airport to reclaim our passports, Boycott was once again ready to play the unofficial knight, and was glad-handing everyone as though it were a benefit match in Ossett. He responded to one enquiry about his welfare by saying he was fit to bat against Trinidad. That idea appealed more than anything.

Like the England players, he missed the airport demonstrators. There were always fewer of them than on little St Vincent a month ago and, though they struck the odd menacing pose and tried to look like the Jets in West Side Story, they were not very threatening. They were quite tuneful though: 'Everybody come protest, protest. Stop this racist tour now ... dem dogs of a-pat-tide, they can run but they can't hide,' and so on.

I felt emboldened to wander past. 'Are you Mr Engel?' said one. 'Yes.' 'Do you support the struggle of the Azanian people?' 'Yes, certainly.' 'Ah, so you think Geoffrey Boycott is a racist dog?' 'Er, that's not what I said.' Indeed, since I have had a bit of fun at Boycott's expense from time to time, I had better say that his demeanour and behaviour throughout this business were splendid. If he got just a little bit ratty on the 937th request for an interview, well, I was beginning to find out how he felt.

I never felt there was that much likelihood of us being

deported once we had made our initial escape from the airport. Boycott had worked out his plans. If the worst came to the worst, he would push off to Miami and have a holiday. 'Marvellous place, Florida,' he said. 'But they don't know who you are,' I protested. 'Last time I was there,' he replied, 'I got stopped in the middle of Disneyland by two Essex supporters and their wives. Right there in Main Street just up from Mickey Mouse's castle. Sums it all up, really.'

GOWER, KNIGHT OF THE NON-NETS
April 1986

Port of Spain: Among other things, yesterday was David Gower's 29th birthday. He marked the occasion by revisiting the sombre scene of England's latest defeat and practising against the bowling machine. He was in his customary good humour: few England captains can have been so impossible to dislike.

On most tours it would be normal to relax after a one-day international prior to strenuous nets today and the start of the Test tomorrow. The atmosphere here is such that journalists are now taking names, and it was noted that only seven of the 17 turned up to use Queen's Park's much criticised facilities yesterday. Hang on a moment, though. The other day the manager said all nets would be compulsory from now on. Absolutely right. There were no compulsory nets yesterday, nor were there optional nets. However, if some of the players want to practise, you can hardly stop them. These were non-nets (non-compulsory), I suppose. This is the world of Milo Minderbinder.

Some people think we are in the world of Cervantes – 'Now idleness triumphed over labour, vice over virtue, presumption over valour and theory over the practice of arms, which only lived in the golden age of knights errant, F. S. Trueman, A. V. Bedser, P. B. H. May' – and if England are three down, then they ought at least to be led by a knight of a sorrowful countenance, not a man who goes around as though cricket tours were still a pleasure.

It has got a bit dotty, but maybe the sorrowful countenance is to hand. No one looked sadder yesterday than Mike Gatting. Once again his thumb was too painful for him to consider trying to bat and his chances of returning for this Test are exceedingly slim. But an ante-post bookmaker might offer a slight shade of odds-on now that Gatting rather than Gower will take England to Australia in six months' time.

That perception could change very rapidly. Gower may command England to victory in the next two Tests; Gatting may not make a run before September. But this winter while Gatting's body has taken a pounding his reputation has remained high. And there was a time last week when his air of bustle, robust purpose and simple determination was right and Gower's sang-froid was wrong. Gower should have tried to practise in Barbados last Friday, if only for show: yesterday was too late. England captains have been crucified in the past – most of them are, in the end – but never before on a sailboard.

Almost certainly, England would still be three down in this series if they were led by a man combining the more relevant qualities of J. M. Brearley and Alexander the Great. But another leader might have sensed the tide of indignation that was flowing in Barbados after the third Test. Two years ago Gower seized his moment in Pakistan when Bob Willis was ill and took control so forcibly that for Willis there was no road back. Now the mood has shifted against his captaincy and Gower was too slow to react. Crisis? What crisis?

It is absurd to blame Gower for the defeat. West Indies have kept winning because their fast bowlers first established a physical domination over the England batsmen, with the bouncers in Kingston, and then turned that into a psychological hold by much less dubious and high quality bowling thereafter. It is improbable that any set of batsmen in the world would have done significantly better. That includes the West Indians; one of the undercurrents of their own cricket is the shortage of high quality young batsmen, Richardson being the great exception – the bowling just grinds them down.

England might have mitigated the disaster by better batting

preparation, determination and leadership. Undoubtedly future tours need to be organised more professionally, with greater attention to every detail from hotel arrangements to coaching. But even if everything had been perfect here, England would still be in the cart.

The easiest reaction to defeats is to change personnel. And at today's selection meeting the omission of Botham may well be seriously discussed for the first time, though it is unlikely to get a majority; I would be surprised if Gower was willing to choose this moment to let Botham's enemies have their triumph. In the medium term, Gower himself must be under threat. Gatting is the only alternative, and it is notable that in the eight consecutive defeats Gower's England have suffered against the West Indies, Gatting has been there to play his role as chief of staff only once.

Gooch has been too preoccupied by his personal troubles to be an adequate substitute. And behind the equivocating statement issued by Lord's yesterday, there appears to be a serious search for a formula that would allow him to leave the tour before the Antigua leg without anyone losing face. That could hardly be a prelude to the captaincy.

Gower has many personal qualities that ought to be of service for years to come; 29 is no age. Would Gatting (two months younger) do any better? In the long run, probably yes. He is more alert, more canny, more up-and-at-'em, more detached on the subject of Botham, and frankly more interested in the job. But, as he said himself when he returned from his nose job, in an uncharacteristically picturesque turn of phrase, he is not a knight on a white charger. Indeed. Sorrowful countenance or not.

DROPPING THE PILOT,
FROM A GREAT HEIGHT
June 1986

Immediately after India's five-wicket win at Lord's yesterday, David Gower was led away to the presentation and television interview, as to the scaffold, though he was still unaware whether he was to be executed or not. At the same moment, Mike Gatting was being intercepted by Peter May, taken into the little physiotherapist's room and offered Gower's job. It was one of the most dramatic moments of the sporting year; and, as with most things in English sport at present, it was utterly botched.

A little later Gower, who now had bruised pride to add to his eye and shoulder injuries, was obliged to sit and answer journalists' questions. He looked utterly worn out, though he maintained the dignity and composure that had been among the hallmarks of his two years in office. Meanwhile, May, chairman of the selectors who made the decision, had sloped off, declining to explain his reasoning or pay Gower any kind of tribute, muttering when cornered: 'It can't be both,' or possibly: 'It can't be Botham.'

Gower is the fourth England captain to be sacked in five years, after Botham (1981), Fletcher (1982) and Willis (1984). There comes a time when the judges ought to be judged, but that never seems to happen. I think the selectors have made the right decision, but it was absolutely insane that it should have hinged, as it must have done, on whether the Indian batting panicked yesterday or the wicket went haywire.

It is almost as ridiculous now that Gatting has been allowed only the two remaining Tests against India, instead of being offered the New Zealand series to give him time to impose his style and show whether or not he is the right man to take England to Australia. If he was worth appointing he was worth appointing properly.

Gower departs the captaincy with what must be regarded as a more dispiriting record than any of his 62 predecessors. Archie MacLaren only won four games, lost 11 and drew seven; Gower has won five, lost 14, and drawn seven. That still looks a bit better than Kapil Dev's score as captain of India; yesterday's victory was his first win in 22 attempts. But Gower is not the worst England captain ever. He did much to improve selection – not the least of his achievements was the rehabilitation of Gatting – and the steering, with Gatting's help, after the confusion of Bob Willis' last few Tests. He has shown much grace under pressure. And he has probably been the best player to captain England since May himself.

The Gatting approach will be different. He will not be afraid to make neo-Churchillian speeches in the dressing-room, the sort of thing Gower would think a bit ridiculous. It will be a more downmarket captaincy. While Gower was Kings, Canterbury, Gatting – 29 last week and an almost exact contemporary as well as friend of Gower – was learning his cricket in suburban Brondesbury with his father acting as club steward. Gower likes fine wines; Gatting likes Branston pickle. He and his wife have never been part of the social set who have dominated English cricket for the past few years. It always looked as though one day Gower would captain England: Gatting would never have got a mention but for the fluke of Emburey going to South Africa in 1982 and losing out on the Middlesex job.

The cricket yesterday had something in common with Willis' last game in charge, when Pakistan beat England in Karachi but made very heavy going of it. India had all day, less 20 minutes lost to early rain, to score 134. They had a couple of moments of anxiety; first at 31 for two, after Srikkanth had been caught at second slip and Gavaskar had gone to one of Downton's most athletic dives; then again at 78 for four after Edmonds had ended another promising performance by Vengsarkar.

England kept pressing, even though both Dilley and Emburey were injured. Azharuddin was run out after a mix-up with Shastri, but Kapil ended any nonsense and won the game with a six into the happy cluster of Indian spectators in the grandstand. One of their banners read, ominously, 'Brownwash'. Ted Dexter, imaginatively, gave the match award to Kapil, whose bowling on Monday was crucial, rather than taking the usual easier route and picking the highest scorer.

This was India's second win in 33 attempts in England (following The Oval in 1971) and only their second over anyone in their last 44. But in Australia last winter they were

79

beaten only by bad weather, and people here have underrated their increasingly efficient and adaptable blend. They won on merit.

WRITING ON THE WALL FOR NORTHAMPTONSHIRE
July 1986

There is a graffito on the back of the players' tea-room at Hastings: Victoria 1066. Since the cricket ground is the only place in town not full of French students, this must have been put there by one of William's soldiers and could well constitute the longest-running gloat in history.

The shortest-running gloat might have come from Northamptonshire after their victory here on Sunday. When the championship match resumed yesterday, their batsmen immediately lurched into the horrors. Here was England batting immediate past (Lamb), present (Larkins) and probably future (Bailey et maybe al).[1] Northamptonshire avoided the follow-on by just three runs, and can expect to be demolished today; Sussex, with seven wickets standing, lead by 320.

The wicket at Priory Meadow is dusty-dry and wise heads have been muttering that the ball has been going through the surface since Saturday. Northamptonshire were bowled out for 136 yesterday, but some of their bowling in both innings may have been less distinguished than their batting. But the batting was woeful enough. The chosen one, Larkins, edged a catch off Imran in the fourth over of the morning without adding to his overnight nine; this score fractionally improves his first class average, now 7.42, though perhaps not his confidence. The dropped one, Lamb, looked far more on terms with himself.

Sussex though, were brooking no nonsense. They no longer have an experienced spinner, but their medium-pacers have made better use than anyone of the pitch's little indentations. There was a troublesome stand between Boyd-Moss and Harper; but then Colin Wells removed them both, and only a few good blows from Nick Cook removed a possible two-day disaster.

When Sussex batted again it was a different game and Imran and Parker stretched their lead towards infinity. This charming and historic ground (Ranji as well as the Conqueror) is still threatened by a new shopping development with C & A replacing c & b. As far as some of the less romantic Northamptonshire players are concerned they can start work now.

[1] Lamb had just been dropped from the Test team, and Larkins surprisingly selected, though he withdrew from the squad before the game.

LAMB LASHES BACK AT SUSSEX
July 1986

Northamptonshire beat Sussex by one wicket at Hastings yesterday. If that makes the cricket sound at least vaguely interesting it can hardly convey the full flavour of a glorious day's play dominated by a glorious century from Allan Lamb.

The victory target was 321, something that was in no one's mind, least of all the Northamptonshire batsmens', when Gould declared overnight to give his men a full day's bowling on this bone dry and unpredictable pitch. But the pitch was nowhere as unpredictable as the game. At various stages, Northamptonshire were one for two, 173 for two, 260 for three, 282 for four, 288 for eight and 301 for nine before the last pair, Walker and Mallender, came together and coolly turned aside the wrath of Imran.

But the climax would have been unthinkable without Lamb. All through the poor run that preceded his exclusion from the Test team, Lamb believed his form was all right; it was his luck that was at fault. Sooner or later, he was bound to ram this theory down someone's throat; in the absence of any visible gin-soaked dodderers, he chose Sussex. Lamb made

157 in three hours with 27 fours. The man England did pick, Larkins, was out second ball for nought, after trying to pull a short ball from Pigott which lifted and gloved him, leaving Larkins with a seasonal average 6.50 and more seriously, a painful bruise on the thumb. Larkins is hopeful he will be fit this morning; but not everyone is so optimistic and he was not a happy man when he left the ground. At least he has not peaked too early.

Lamb said later that Northamptonshire could easily have been all out for 100. His team was staring at defeat when ball, pitch, Imran and Pigott were all at their freshest and most lethal. On Monday Sussex had bowled them out for 136 and the wicket had got no easier.

Lamb was brilliant. Some of his early shots may have been born of desperation, but they succeeded so well on the fast, sloping outfield that the Sussex attack lost its direction. Then Lamb took complete command, with hard, chopped, pull strokes and brutally struck square-cuts and drives. He almost got a century before lunch. It came just afterwards, in 105 minutes; and though Lamb slowed up afterwards and gave a hard chance on 129, the innings had now obtained grandeur and Northamptonshire were thinking of victory. If anyone bats better all summer, I only hope I am there to see it.

Capel was Lamb's first admirable and admiring supporter. Then Bailey, whacking the ball off the front foot – in one case whacking it over long-on, the stands and almost into the Free Christian Church – hit 57 in 75 minutes. The batsmen were cruising but all game there had been movement off the seam; Lamb had just been too good to notice. But after he went the middle order collapsed to Colin Wells, who took four wickets in five overs including Harper, leg-before first ball.

Suddenly, Sussex were favourites again. But Wild pushed the score past 300 before driving to mid-off, leaving the stage for Walker and Mallender, both Yorkshire-born seamers, to play Hirst and Rhodes in the final act. The last eight runs all came in singles.

Somewhere far away, the TCCB were mulling over Botham and the game's troubles yet again. This was cricket somewhere near to perfection, with sun and sea breezes and the gulls wheeling round the castle ruins. Even the gatemen were friendly; Lord's might regard that as bringing their version of the game into disrepute.

To be absolutely right, the game should have been a tie; but that happened on Sussex's annual visit here two years ago and Hastings people might regard another as a bit routine. It was also unfortunate that yesterday's *Guardian* misquoted the Conqueror's pavilion graffito 'Victoire 1066' as 'Victoria'; everything here was magnifique, mais ce n'est pas la gare.

BOTHAM'S HISTORICAL ROMANCE
August 1986

This is an attempt at a true account of events at The Oval yesterday, but I cannot entirely be certain any of this really happened. On the face of it, the final Test of the summer went along the same dingy way as the last two games. New Zealand plodding their weary way to 142 for four before the rain set in.

But one amazing cricketer transcended the day as he has transcended so many others. Ian Botham equalled Dennis Lillee's wicket-taking record with his first ball back in Test cricket after his drug-induced suspension, and beat it in the next over. He finished the day with three for 36. No one predicted that: even Botham at his most crowing would never have dared. When did any team game ever produce such a sub-plot as this?

Play had started late, the opening overs had proceeded peacefully enough, it was time for a bowling change. Up trots Botham. His loosener was intended as such, hardly more than a long hop. But Bruce Edgar, transfixed by the leg-end more than the ball, or perhaps just anxious to play a bit-part in history, waved his bat and helped it to second slip. The crowd erupted. Botham erupted, made a series of gestures that indicated he was quite pleased with himself and embraced Gatting as though they were long-lost twin brothers, which in a way they are. Amid the scrum of players Gooch asked: 'Who writes your bloody script then?' If it comes from a comic strip, it is from a new one: Ian of the Clichés or the Wizard of Ego.

Botham came into this match with a post-comeback bowling average of 131.5. For pointless hours in Antigua, Botham bowled and bowled in an attempt to get that wicket. Now one suspension, four months and a million column inches later he had done it at the first attempt. Don't ask for a cricketing explanation: there is none. We are into the paranormal.

He almost broke the record next ball. It was a beauty, which Jeff Crowe had to play though it slithered off the edge boot-high to Emburey at third slip, who was a fraction too slow and it trickled for four.

Botham's third ball was a good bouncer: his eighth almost sliced back onto Crowe's stumps: his 12th caught Crowe square, slipped past a half-cock defensive shot and took him on the pad. Some thought it might have missed leg stump, but umpire Shepherd's hesitation may have come simply because he did not believe it either. That was the record.

On a cloudy morning, the atmosphere offered help as did the bouncy pitch, which is what Gatting hoped for when he chose an attacking line-up (leaving out Willey) and made New Zealand bat. Dilley and Small bowled well without much luck, as Emburey did later. But throughout Botham's first spell, he bowled with as much genuine swing and vigour as at any time in the past four confused seasons: and that came from the heart, not the wicket.

After lunch, Martin Crowe drove down the wrong line at Dilley and was leg-before. Botham came back for his second spell with the New Zealand captain Coney convinced that the bowling was there to be taken. He lofted Small for a six over the long-off boundary and whenever he saw a chance against Botham, he took it. Back went the fielders for the mistimed hook. On rushed Coney, 39 off 38 balls, while Wright dug himself into the trenches at the other end. In came another attempted bouncer, Coney went for the hook and the ball flew high off the splice and down into Gooch's grasp at second slip.

'A medium-pacer in fast bowlers' clothes,' Coney was heard

to mutter to the incoming batsman Gray as they passed. Gray will get a chance to test that theory today, though he does not deserve it: he was dropped twice in successive overs while on seven – horribly, by Edmonds at mid-on, then more forgivably by Lamb at silly point.

The rain arrived just after tea, and the crowd drifted away. They had seen what they needed to see. Coney, like so many of the 356 previous victims, the administrators, the commentators and the Press were left behind still feeling bemused. Botham has still not proved that he can ever again be an ox-strong, all-day, England bowler. Eleven overs in a cool English August is no guide to what might happen in 105 degrees at Adelaide. He has provided further evidence that he is the most fascinating un-writeoffable character that this fascinating game has ever produced. Above everything else, perhaps, this was his tryst with destiny. He met it, as ever, head on and came off best. As Botham will tell you, you cannot believe everything you read in the papers. But you had better believe this: the man is back.

AUSTRALIANS CLOSE THEIR EYES TO IGNOMINY
December 1986

Melbourne: The Australian sporting public has a marvellous knack of averting its gaze from things it doesn't like. In just 40 minutes after tea in Melbourne yesterday Australia lost their last five wickets, culminating in the catch by Gladstone Small that won the Ashes again for England. Long before then, the crowd – though 23,000 of them were physically present – had given up on the cricket and devoted itself to cheering the flashes of Davis Cup news from up the road. The rest of Australia was even less bothered. One of their ghastliest defeats in 110 years of Test cricket hardly got a mention on the evening news bulletins amid the orgy of tennis self-congratulation. Anyone for cricket?

England's win, by an innings and 14, gave them a 2-0 lead in the series with the Sydney Test to come, keeps the Ashes at home for another two and a half years and ensures that one of English cricket's most fraught years ends in triumph.

In Jamaica 10 months ago England lost the first Test of 1986 inside three days. Now they have won inside three days, the first time they have done that in Australia for 84 years. Mike Gatting, who will remember Jamaica for his smashed nose, has finished the year as the eighth captain this century (after Warner, Douglas, Chapman, Jardine, Hutton, Illingworth and Brearley) to bring the Ashes home and only the third (after Douglas and Gower) to put Australia in to bat and win.

And Gladstone Small, who only a week ago was the poor sap bowling into the gale in Tasmania, was named as man of the match, for his first-day bowling, two more important wickets yesterday and his all-round enthusiasm. England can never have had a more improbable match-winner. He was only the narrowest of last-minute choices to play ahead of Foster when Dilley pulled out. Technically, he should never have been allowed to play for England in the first place because he arrived from Barbados after the official cut-off point of his 14th birthday. He appeared before the Registration Committee as a teenager wearing specs and his customary hunch and, after everyone had made the usual whispered jokes about him leaving the coathanger inside his suit, the committee gave him a special dispensation, convinced he was entirely committed to England rather than the West Indies. They were dead right: he is the most wholehearted trier in the business, and suddenly he is a star. 'I'm very glad for Glad,' said Gatting in one of his more felicitous phrases.

Everyone is glad for Gatting too. By spirit and example rather than strategy, he has been a fine leader of a team that has survived a dreadful start by seizing the key points of the series, the opening days of Brisbane and Melbourne, like an élite army unit staging a surprise *coup d'état*.

If the applause is muted, it is because the opposition has been so wretched, so hopelessly windblown too. After their bowling inadequacies were exposed earlier in the series, Australia gambled this time by dropping a batsman. The bowlers did reasonably well on Saturday. Yesterday the batting fell apart once more, this time to 194 all out. Yet again the end of Border, after they had reached a solid 113 for two, was the end of Australia. Both Border and the Australian manager, Bob Simpson, said they had opposed the selectors' decision to drop Greg Ritchie, leaving only four specialist bats. Even Gatting said he was surprised by that. Six weeks ago, it was Border who was being puzzled by the opposition, when England forswore practice two days before the opening Test and the whole team wore a distracted, fragmented look.

Well, they've all gone quiet over there. Border was quiet yesterday, upset by the team's failure to build on a hopeful tour of India and admitting that he did not know where Australia went from here. He did not advocate wholesale sackings and did not contemplate resignation. 'We're doing so many little things badly. The talent is there, that's the disappointing thing. We're just not doing it. I can't quite put my finger on why. I'm determined to see it out and hopefully things will improve.'

Indeed it was Gatting, having used the world 'tremendous' nine times in a two-minute interview with Tony Greig (which he is entitled to do), who hinted at the darkest thoughts, admitting that he had not enjoyed the captaincy a lot of the time, which is understandable. He enjoyed yesterday, though, and started by taking the first two catches himself at first slip. Australia began their second innings 208 behind. The trouble began almost at once when Boon failed for the seventh time out of eight in the series. Counting the Tasmania match, it was the fourth time in eight days that he has donated a catch to the England slip cordon.

England bump off captains at regular intervals, but being Australia's vice-captain is dodgier than being manager of Wolves. Boon is the fifth in Border's 25 Tests as captain (after Hogg, Hilditch, Hookes and Bright), and there may well be a sixth at Sydney.

Jones went likewise, off a confused square-cut. But while Border and Marsh were together Australia breathed easily.

On seven, Border reached 6,807 Test runs and displaced Ken Barrington from the all-time top 10. The video screen flashed the message, the crowd applauded, Border took no notice. He really does care more about his team than his records. On 32, Border joined Gower in passing 1,000 Test runs for the calendar year, which is a comment more on the fixture list than anything else. On 34, the important thing happened: Small tempted him into the drive, Emburey snaffled the slip catch.

Australia's downhill progress was so relentless that Ritchie or anyone could hardly have made much difference. There were even two run-out mix-ups, both involving Waugh. Marsh got stranded, first on 60 (after staying another three and a half hours to take his batting time for the tour to almost 35 hours) and then in mid-pitch. Sleep was so far out of his ground that even a bad throw by Gower left Edmonds time and a half to knock the bails off. Matthews was bowled off his pads not offering a stroke and so the horrors rolled on for Australia.

One wicket gave special satisfaction: Zoehrer's dismissal at short leg off Edmonds. Zoehrer, who has had a very ragged match behind the stumps and is probably still unfit, apparently started a sledging match with Edmonds on Saturday evening, which sounds like the kettle getting in before the pot. This was part of a general outbreak of nostalgia for the 1970s, the heyday of cricketing hooliganism, with McDermott marking his wickets with stomping and gesticulation, and England greeting a turned-down bat-pad decision (on Marsh just before he was out) with complete dumb insolence.

This must have all spread from the tennis courts. By now the crowd were even booing when the scoreboard switched back from the tennis score to the cricket, but Australia's end was so rapid it was almost painless. When Hughes was last out, Gatting, in a gesture of pure charm and friendship, was met by the overthrown king, Gower, with a broad grin and an outstretched hand.

PAKISTAN'S CENTURIONS ON THE MARCH
August 1987

Test matches at The Oval often have a dreamlike quality: high scores on torpid late summer days. There were times yesterday when Mike Gatting must have felt he was having one of those nightmares when you urgently want to scream and can't quite manage it.

After two days' play Pakistan have reached 616 for six, and Imran evidently intends to bat on this morning. They could easily score 700,[1] maybe they will meet the FT Index on the way down. England would them be forced to make 500-odd to avoid the follow-on. The wicket was perfect yesterday, but it may not stay that way and England do not look in a heroic-rearguard frame of mind. As they trudged off they looked in slightly better condition than an army retreating from Moscow, but only slightly.

Three wickets fell during the day: Salim Malik was out for 102, Javed Miandad for 260 and Imran, playing almost certainly his last Test innings,[2] for 118. We are, as they say, talking telephone numbers. Javed's double century was never in doubt. Much of the time the main question was whether he would make a triple century and maybe even pass Len Hutton's 364, made 49 years ago, which the rickety scoreboard on the Harleyford Road side no doubt clanked up just the same. England were 634 for five after two days of that Test; Pakistan just failed to match that.

Javed is not one of those players who decides he has made enough and gives his wicket away. As a teenager, he scored 311 for Karachi Whites against the National Bank in one of those charmingly bizarre Pakistani domestic fixtures, and this was his fourth 200 in Tests. He batted wonderfully again yesterday, though he became understandably tired in the end (he batted for 10 hours 25 minutes in all) and was stranded on 253 while Imran charged from 57 to 101.

Technically, England bowled a bit better than they did on Thursday. Emburey, in particular, was more accurate though he failed to end his melancholy record of not taking a wicket all series. Botham conceded 180 runs but was tireless and

Dilley rather heroic considering his ankle was still playing up. Once in a while the ball beat the bat. Pakistan might also have been bothered by the scoreboard showing 555, quintuple Nelson; or by the first outbreak of Mexican waving this summer; or by the crowd throwing apples into the outfield.

On second thoughts, they were used to that. And England were in such disarray there was nothing to be done. Foster's injury kept him out all day and even Broad, whose bowling was not required but whose batting definitely will be, somehow acquired a groin strain and disappeared for a time. By mid-afternoon Moxon and Gatting were bowling. On the 1984-85 tour of India David Gower was asked why he never gave Moxon a bowl. 'Cos I've seen him,' he said.

The first landmark was Salim Malik's 100. His batting was more pushy than in the past this series. He began the day by scoring 12 off Dilley's first over, reached his hundred in four and a half hours and re-established himself among the leaders of the Crowe/Hick/Dean Jones/Azharuddin generation of world batsmen before he gave a catch to point off Botham. There may be young Englishmen of a similar calibre, but they hardly get picked.

Javed's batting was more fitful than on Thursday, but some of his back-foot shots were again delicious – little more than whisks, perfectly timed. I suspect his mastery only faltered when his mind wandered.

It was a stupendous innings, but he only overshadowed his captain in quantity. Imran came in before lunch and, third ball, lifted Emburey over the top for six. All along people have been cynical about Imran's stated intentions of going all out for victory this match. This was his earnest proof that he meant business. It was only his fourth Test hundred but it was a reprise of all the skills that have been submerged beneath his fast bowling. A great talent is departing the cricketing stage.

Between 2.35 on Thursday and 5.10 yesterday only one wicket fell. The Javed-Malik fourth-wicket stand of 234 set a new Pakistan v England record; the Javad-Imran fifth wicket stand of 191 almost did the same. In the six sessions the run-rate was remarkably consistent – 95, 111, 91, 109, 94, 116

– but in the last hour, two wickets fell. Dilley took the third new ball and beat Javed three times in two overs. These were two weary men, like bare-knuckle prizefighters approaching the umpteenth round, and Dilley at long last got the knockdown when Javed drove the return catch.

Half an hour later Imran was run out, attempting a fourth at the instigation of the fleet-footed Ijaz, through good work by Radford and Botham. But even these England successes were not that bad for Pakistan; Javed was starting to think of milestones rather than quick runs and Imran needs to be fresh for bowling. Poor England have been buffeted more by fate than anything else these past two days. But somehow one feels that if Gatting had won the toss, the scoreboard would not look quite as devastating as this. Pakistan are a formidably determined side.

[1] 708, actually.
[2] Not quite, as it turned out.

A NATION'S DREAM IS DASHED TO EARTH
November 1987

Lahore: To the amazement of a nation, indeed two nations, Australia beat Pakistan by 18 runs in Lahore yesterday to reach the World Cup final. Though the finish was not exceptionally close, the occasion was one of the most extraordinary I have witnessed. The Pakistanis elevated this tournament into something above and beyond mere sport, and they thus fell to earth with a mighty thud. The result will enhance their cricketing reputation, forged in the three previous World Cups and countless Test series, for faltering at crucial moments.

It is not easy to square it with Australia's recent, much-battered, reputation, but they go into Sunday's final in tremendous spirits. Allan Border said he was ecstatic. Under pressure he admitted that, with the final in Calcutta, he wanted England rather than India to win the second semi-final today. The cards fell in Australia's direction from the start. Border wanted desperately to win the toss, bat first, get off to a good start, and put the opposition under pressure, and so it was. Australia scored 267 for eight: Pakistan, daunted by this, made mistakes right away and were soon 38 for three. The task was just too much.

The difference between the teams can be calibrated exactly. After 49 overs both teams had 249; Pakistan, however, were all out off the last ball of the 49th. Australia faced one last over from Saleem Jaffar, who had a nightmare: Steve Waugh hit him for 18, with Jaffar reduced to bowling full-tosses as a defensive measure.

The over before that had been even more extraordinary. Imran, bowling, so he insists, for the last time in international cricket, produced a quite exceptional wicket maiden: fast, accurate, penetrating, and almost unplayable.

The 40,000 crowd, while this was happening, were making so much noise that umpire Bird could not hear the new batsman ask for his guard. Much of the row came from the segregated women's enclosure where the supposedly demure ladies of Islam, waving banners and cheerleaders' pom-poms, maintained a ferocious din for three-quarters of the game. One quickly realised, arriving shortly after sunrise with the ground already packed, that this was not the second day of Derbyshire v Leicestershire. But Pakistan's later wickets fell amid a silence more profound than at any county match: not a hand clapped, not a dog barked. When it was all over, a man in the Press box burst into uncontrollable sobs.

Suddenly Pakistan are no longer co-hosts or even participants, and Imran is no longer an international cricketer – unless the bitterness of this failure makes him anxious to carry on and forget it. He performed sensationally again yesterday (his final five-over spell during the slog produced figures of 5-1-17-3) but it was less than inspired of him to let Jaffar, who had been hopelessly off-line throughout, bowl the final over.

Jaffar's waywardness gave Australia their early impetus. Marsh and the in-form Boon put on 73, only their fourth-biggest opening partnership in seven games. Jones looked good too, until he was bowled attempting a cut of uncharacteristic inelegance. Border misfired again after seeing a mere third of the strike in a 10-over stand with the nondescript but effective Veletta.

At 155 for one after 31 overs, Australia were contemplating an enormous score. Slowly their expectations dropped away. First Imran came back. Then there was a most curious run-out when O'Donnell was ruled out by umpire Shepherd even though he was safe in his own ground: Waugh at the time was past him (he was walking back to the pavilion) and so they were deemed to have crossed. It was lucky for Australia that Waugh was allowed to stay: it is unlikely that any of their other late batsmen could have dealt with Jaffar half as effectively.

Pakistan's innings was always ill-starred. Rameez was run out after only three balls; Mansoor drove down the wrong line; Malik was caught at mid-off, Javed and Imran did an impressive restoration job, but there was a great deal to restore. Javed, the heir-presumptive to the captaincy, played a strange innings – mature, almost subdued for the most part, mixed in with occasional dashes of the utterly original. After Imran went, he tried to hang around while the hitters did their stuff. Akram struck two sixes, one of which almost struck the cup itself, on its display podium behind long-on. If you can't win it, wreck it.

Nothing worked. The Pakistanis locked themselves in their dressing-room; the Australians flew straight on to India. They say they aren't surprised. Hmmm. Australian television is not even scheduled to show the final.

THE BEGGARS' OPERA
November 1987

Calcutta: Something quite remarkable has happened over here, and it is not just that England and Australia are contesting the World Cup final. Calcutta has been given a wash and brush-up for the occasion, and although not exactly convincing it is undeniably impressive. About 800 beggars and street people have been either run out of town or locked up. And everything within sight of the Eden Gardens stadium or the Grand Hotel, the teams' headquarters, has been refurbished, painted and sanitised.

The main street, Chowringhee, used to have a vast shanty town centred just across the road from the Grand's entrance. Since West Bengal has a Marxist government, one might have imagined that the Grand would have gone by now to be replaced by a People's Liberation Commissariat or something. Instead the shanty town has gone, to be replaced by saplings and cream-coloured balustrades designed to create the flavour of the Esplanade at Frinton. Suddenly it has become possible to absorb the crumbling, romantic dignity of the 19th-century buildings and the names – Cuthbertson and Harper, the Café Monico, the Italian stores, all built in a style blending Glasgow and Naples – without being constantly brought back to earth by the terrifying vigour of life at ground level. 'Commit no nuisance. By order,' says a sign. It is not a very fair instruction.

No city has gone to such lengths to put up a front for a mere sporting event since the Russians virtually depopulated Moscow for the 1980 Olympics. And this is for just one day's cricket. After all their efforts, it is rather sad that it is not the one day's cricket Calcutta wanted. 'An England-Australia clash could catch anyone's imagination anywhere,' wrote a local paper man sadly, 'but not this time, not in Calcutta.'

The black market for tickets appears to have collapsed with the Indian batting on Thursday. A Bengali Flash Stan pleaded with me yesterday to buy two good seats at face value. There was even the odd spare seat on the flight here, which is unheard of in India.

But the show goes on, and how. At Eden Gardens, always an imposing arena, they were putting the last touches yesterday to the work that makes it the world's greatest cricket ground by a mile. It is now almost Olympian in its splendour, with flamboyant fibreglass roofing, a spanking new pavilion with executive boxes for the Calcutta money men, an

94

air-conditioned Press centre, an enormous electronic scoreboard, and seats for about 96,000 people, more than attended the three finals at Lord's put together. All of this has apparently been done without a rupee's worth of assistance from the government. And people in England prattle on about the importance of preserving the slummy old Oval.

The old Ranji stand, where 16 people were killed during a soccer stampede seven years ago, has been demolished. Happily, however, the advertisements for 'Tosh's Teas' have survived. And there is still amid the splendour a certain, shall we say, Indian-ness. The soldiers who were extremely anxious to keep me off the grass in front of the pavilion were not in the least bothered when I wandered out to the wicket. And round the ground yesterday there were seven digital clocks showing the time in each of the World Cup countries with the sole exception of India, which could make the umpires' job difficult. 'It should be there,' said a puzzled official.

Time is of the essence in this match. In Calcutta there is only just enough time between morning dew and evening twilight to get in a 50-over cricket match. When New Zealand played Zimbabwe last week (and 55,000 turned up for that, so the ground is not going to be deserted tomorrow) they lopped 10 minutes off the lunch interval just to be certain. They will not be playing on until 8.43 p.m. in this contest, as they did at Lord's in 1975.

As they are whisked between the Grand and the ground the players and dignitaries will be amazed at this well-groomed city. It is almost a relief to report that behind this parade-ground facade, life in Calcutta is continuing pretty much as normal. In the back streets just a few minutes away the passing show is as vivid as ever: goatherds, rickshaw-wallahs, money-changers, wandering holy men, street barbers, human pack-horses, the lot.

I watched a man slowly trying to pick a living from a rubbish tip, and at night the city still belongs to the street-sleepers and Calcutta's real guardians, the rats. In the shadows, it is not easy to tell the difference immediately between the sleekest rats and the most pathetic humans.

Clean-up or no clean-up, I still counted 50 people asleep on one small stretch of pavement. And next week, no doubt, the beggars will be back. If England win, if Australia win, even if India had won, life for them goes on much the same.

WALKING BACK TO GODLINESS
April 1988

Lunel, France: Malcolm Muggeridge is supposed to have said that a man ultimately has to decide to be either a saint or a sod. Ian Botham has not quite made up his mind yet. He is, however, not mucking about with the messy grey areas in between.

Botham yesterday completed Stage Five of his elephantine Tour de France, a venture which may ultimately raise £3 million for research into leukaemia. He has already walked 116 miles and shrugged off the furore at the start of the epic about the small matter of a headlock on a fellow airline passenger to whom he had not been formally introduced. No one seems to have any doubt, least of all Botham, that he will emulate Hannibal, cross the Alps, and take Italy by storm. In essence, this megastunt is great-hearted, magnificent, and beyond criticism. Unfortunately, it is quite hard work getting to the essence: a dozen people trying their damnedest to walk between Perpignan and Turin, 440 miles in three weeks, for a vital charity.

Surrounding them is the most bizarre retinue even Botham has ever collected. There is the usual core cast: family, nanny, Andy the genial gopher, David the court jester, Chris the ghost writer – everyone except the lawyer, and I bet he isn't far away. But as well as them you have two remaining elephants, now used mainly for symbolic appearances, not unhappy but a little bewildered. There are a couple of serious students of Carthaginian history who hoped to make a proper reconstruction of Hannibal's trek and are now even more bewildered than the elephants, who are at least used to circus life.

There are a zillion media men, including five television crews, none of them conspicuously understaffed; a fluctuating group of celebrity droppers-in, headed this weekend by Jim Capaldi, a rock singer not in the first flush of fame, and Eddie Edwards, said to be a skier; and there are the organisers, some of whom evidently specialise in the arcane art of anti-public relations. And then there are the 40 million extras – the population of France, sometimes meeting and greeting, occasionally applauding, more often getting angry because of the delays to traffic, most often ignoring yet another manifestation of English insanity. This is a nation which probably thinks that Headingley '81 is an obscure sort of white burgundy.

There is not even a serious attempt to involve the French. It is illegal to raise money along the road here, so there can be none of the spontaneous outpouring of joy and generosity that surrounded Botham's first walk from John O'Groats to Land's End. The money raised, over £1 million on the most cautious estimates, has come in through sponsorship schemes in Britain, mainly organised by General Portfolio. This turns out to be an insurance company rather than one of Hannibal's Carthaginian sidekicks.

A few French people know what is going on. '*Bon courage,*' shouted one motorist yesterday. Two old men of the traditional pastis-drinking class were overheard in a bar as the entourage passed by. '*Les Anglais?*' asked one. '*Les Anglais,*' confirmed his friend. '*Les Anglais sont fous,*' said the first.

The walk yesterday went 25 miles on a grey, drizzly day between the small towns of Mereval and Lunel through the flat, turgid countryside of southern Languedoc. We went past wintry vines, barking dogs, dead cats, discarded Gauloises packets, a few Van Goghian cypress trees, and a good many malevolent Easter motorists.

There was yet again no doubt about the stage winner: Botham arrived in Lunel in his blue tracksuit, not quite daisy fresh but full of beans nonetheless and totally buoyant. Everything was wonderful: the reaction had been marvellous and the Italians, he had been told, were going ape about the whole idea. And he was looking forward to the Alps next week: 'It will be a change of scenery, and you use different muscles going uphill.' He is a demon walker. Every day Botham sets an astonishing pace of around four miles an hour. The great advantage of staying with him is that he is in front of the elephants, so you don't have to skirt round jumbo-sized droppings.

But only cheats and irregulars can normally keep up. The other regulars are strung out miles behind – including Botham's wife Kathy and, even further behind, his former Queensland team-mate Greg Ritchie, puffing the occasional fag, heavily sponsored in Australia to stay the course, utterly determined not to let anyone down but quite clearly struggling. He is amazed by Botham. 'I've been rooming with him all season,' said Ritchie. 'He's done no walking at all. Then he comes here and goes off, whoosh. The man's unbelievable. He's a freak.' Certainly, no one observing Botham here could ever go along with the customary cricket writers' claptrap about his lack of fitness.

Kath's performance has, in its way, been even more heroic. She is no professional athlete, and has done astonishingly well to get this far. Yesterday she had to be helped over the last three miles. She has groin strains and back pains, and if she goes on she's potty. All along she has nothing going for her except the extraordinary quiet tenacity which has preserved her marriage. You have to admit they are quite a family.

But as Botham himself said: 'Wherever I go, whatever I do, there is always some joker trying to bring me down.' There is, and his name's Ian. It does require an enormous effort to get bad publicity from an event like this. But he did it. It was not all his fault. We all know what the tabloids are like, and there are some right jumped-up jobsworths round here to make things worse. But Botham's own gift for doing the near-impossible is, of course, matchless. The sacking by Queensland is a personal disaster which may well cost him almost as much money as he is raising for leukaemia. 'The thing about Ian,' a team-mate told me once, 'is that he believes doing one great thing cancels out all the little shitty ones.' Maybe he should now walk across Australia.

We know Botham can raise money for this worthy cause.

The task of restoring his own earning potential is, however, now Himalayan rather than Alpine. Two other state teams, South Australia and Victoria, have been vaguely linked with him, but both seem implausible given the circumstances of his dismissal by Queensland. Botham's position in England seems secure, at least until he screws up again. Phil Neale, the Worcestershire captain, who walked here for two days and flew home with relief, is still captivated by the man. England, after their dreadful winter, are unlikely to reject anyone who has the remotest chance of helping them against the West Indies.

But Botham is now saying he would much rather stay at home in the winter: feet up in front of the fire and the odd walk – the dog across the dales, for sure, but maybe too the Napoleonic route from Paris to Moscow or the Great Wall of China. The Great Wall I can believe; the feet up is the unlikely bit. When Hannibal ran out of options to avoid his enemies, he poisoned himself – a course I do not recommend. But if Australia is out then Botham has only one option to make big money for himself as well as sick kids: South Africa. If he were to play there, after all he has said on the subject, he would finally settle the Muggeridgean question. He would be a sod.

GATTING'S CITY HONOUR NOT WITHOUT PROFIT
June 1988

The omens for the cricket match yesterday could hardly have been less auspicious. First, it was chucking with rain though that's not so unusual in this climate. Secondly, the star of the show had just been sacked as England captain after supposed saucy goings-on had got into the papers. On reflection, that's not so unusual either.

The occasion was a six-a-side competition at the ground of the Honorable Artillery Company in the City of London to raise money for Mike Gatting in his benefit year. It did that all right: the bat he used in the Trent Bridge Test was auctioned for £400 – more than some old-time county beneficiaries made all year – and there were estimates that the day may have netted £20,000. But it did more than that; it cheered him up. 'I was a bit apprehensive about coming today,' said Gatting. 'I didn't know what sort of reception I'd get. But everyone's been absolutely brilliant.'

Actually, the guests were shocked – but by the sacking, not the supposed goings-on. They were all City types, taking time off from life on the cutting edge of booming Britain. 'Perhaps we're not typical newspaper readers here,' said someone over lunch. 'We're broadminded in the City. And we understand that people who work hard also play hard.' One banker compared the Test and County Cricket Board with the Securities and Investments Board, which is seen in the City as the epitome of ineffectual bossiness. He knew no greater insult.

When Gatting was introduced over lunch, the 400 present cheered. When the organiser, Mr Jeremy Bond, chairman of the marketing firm Moorgate, said he hoped Gatting would be captain again for the third Test I thought for a moment that the assembled company might get up and march on Lord's.

But this is England. And anyway, everyone was much too busy enjoying the experience of a lunch interval lasting until after 4 p.m. Just like the old days pre-Big Bang, if it is polite to use such a phrase in a cricketing context.

The celebrity professionals present included John Emburey who was summoned to Lord's in mid-morning to be handed the poisoned chalice. 'I don't know whether to congratulate you or commiserate,' said Mike Gatting's wife Elaine on his return. There was also the Australian captain, Allan Border, who wore the traditional colonial air of bewilderment when confronted with inexplicable English behaviour. 'I don't think this could have happened anywhere else,' said Border. 'In Australia we don't have papers behaving like that. And if we did I would expect the Board to back me. What they said to Gatting was: "We believe you but you're sacked." It's astonishing.'

100

The City view was much the same. If Lord's plc was a quoted company, everyone would have been rushing to sell. 'You'd have to ask questions about a chairman who had sacked four managing directors,' said one broker.

But cricket is a minor diversion to these people. The memory that will linger for many is of the ground, an oasis of green on the edge of the square mile. Had Henry VIII not granted it to the Artillerymen in perpetuity, it would now be worth about £1 billion on the property market. I saw several men in sharp suits staring out longingly from the champagne tent as the game proceeded in the drizzle. They were not contemplating the follies of the past 48 hours nor even reminiscing, rheumy-eyed, about the eccentric old game in the way Englishmen do. In the mind's eye they were building office blocks.

A DAY AT FINCHAMPSTEAD
June 1988

In answer to the first question, Finchampstead is a village south of Wokingham near Berkshire's border with Hampshire. In answer to the second question, Berkshire were playing Yorkshire in the opening round of the NatWest Trophy. In answer to the third question, alas they didn't. Not even close.

Instead, Yorkshire managed the seventh 10-wicket win in the competition's 26 seasons. They were chasing only 105 and the game was over by 4 p.m. without the Yorkshire captain Phil Carrick acquiring a single extra fleck of grey.

Yet all season Yorkshire have been wandering round the first class circuit like a mobile crisis. Suddenly against this band of amateurs they were able to flex their muscles and imagine there were an old-fashioned Yorkshire side. The part of Len Hutton was played by Metcalfe, Wilfred Rhodes by Carrick, and Fred Trueman and Bill Bowes by Jarvis and Fletcher, the man of the match. Normal unsuccessful business will probably be resumed at Hove on Saturday.

This was merely an extreme example of almost every game between the first class counties and the best of the rest since knock-out cricket began 25 years ago. It even happens when the Minor Counties play as a unit fielding mostly old pros. Indeed, Berkshire's two ex-first class players had as hard a time as everyone else. Graham Roope, who played 21 Tests in the 1970s, batted long enough to avoid the possibility of a pre-lunch finish. But since he took 33 overs scoring 21, at one time had 45 runless minutes and later limped off the field having turned his ankle, he did not exactly glitter. Meanwhile, the off-spinner Peter Lewington, who once played for Warwickshire, was clouted for two successive sixes by Metcalfe.

Why is it the same story, year after year, 15 or 16 games out of 16? Roope reckons it is a matter of practice and professionalism. The basics of one-day cricket become second nature to county players: alertness in the field, nudging and nurdling singles, bowling four testing, swinging balls an over rather than two. It seems to me also that professionals, having learned cricket, then unlearn a great deal to play the one-day game. In contrast, Berkshire's top scorer Mark Stear blocked and drove absolutely classically but had no idea how to score quickly enough to put Yorkshire under pressure.

Berkshire could hardly blame the pitch. It was made for batting – and in a sense did their cricket more credit than the kind of minefield on which they might have fluked a victory.

Finchampstead is only a village but its cricket shows what can be achieved with an enthusiastic committee and an able groundsman. True, it is the sort of village where the rustics have long since beaten their ploughshares into season tickets to London. But it could easily stage an efficient and lasting three-day match, which is more than can be said for places like ... well, Headingley, actually.

In the sunshine it looked handsome too. As a day out for the bank managers, as an affirmation of the game's national character, as an encouragement to harassed Yorkshiremen, Finchampstead was a huge success. As a game of cricket, it was silly.

HICK: SIX AND OUT IN FRONT

August 1988

August, as the Welsh sage Don Shepherd put it, is the blackmail month. In other words, teams with no chance of winning the championship can set the contenders ridiculous targets in the knowledge that they will chase anything and quite likely lose. But with Graeme Hick around, Worcestershire can meet even the most outrageous ransom demands. They had to score 341 in four hours to beat Glamorgan at Abergavenny yesterday and did it. Well anyway, Hick did it: he made 159 of them.

Worcestershire won by five wickets with four balls to spare and thus displaced Kent at the top of the table, reclaiming the position they lost on 21 June. If they are to be caught again, I fancy it will take a team with more firepower than Kent to do it. And, despite the injuries among their bowlers, they will take some catching – in Hick they have one of the wonders of the age. On 79 he reached his 2,000 for the season. With five games to go he will probably pass 2,500 which has only been done once (by Gooch) since the championship programme was reduced 20 years ago. The second-best young batsman on the circuit, Matthew Maynard, also made a hundred yesterday, and in only 84 minutes. But it was a cheapo – made against Home Guard bowlers such as Neale and Curtis as Worcestershire goaded Glamorgan towards a declaration.

The chase might have been over before it started. The opener, Lord, was out quickly and Greg Thomas almost held onto a hard return catch when Hick was four. But he didn't. From then on Hick was the perfect master. I think he may have played and missed at one in the 20s; he definitely gave a stinging half-chance on the boundary on 135 before ultimately being caught at long-on. But it was the innings of a young man who has already found the answer to a game that everyone else finds puzzling, and wonders what the fuss is about. Before long they ought to invent new rules for him, three extra stumps maybe or one-hand, one-bounce or the old back-garden rule of six and out.

Hick hit five sixes yesterday. I do not think any of them

actually splashed into the brook behind the sightscreen at the Pennypound End as one of Maynard's did. But one made it into the blackberry bushes; another hit the roof of a house behind long-on which, according to Abergavenny folklore, was long occupied by a man who always refused to give the ball back, and one of his straight hits may have landed in England. There were 15 fours as well, and the 61 he scored after his century only took 35 balls. This was Hick's seventh century of the summer, his 15th since this time last year and, including one-day games, he has scored 2,912 runs so far this season. He is alive and playing county cricket in this Year of Disgrace 1988 and he has to be seen to be believed.

Mind you, the Glamorgan attack trying its hardest was not vastly different from Worcestershire mucking about. Shastri was absent wounded and, with so little pace in the wicket, there was nothing in it for Thomas, who had to retreat after being struck for 32 in two overs. Glamorgan's other senior seamer Barwick had an even greater humiliation: wicket-keeper Metson stood up to him.

But the target was enormous, and if Hick had got out even 10 minutes earlier Worcestershire would almost certainly have failed. Curtis, England's current opener but doomed to play Sancho Panza when he bats for his county, made 86. The in-form Neale scored 51. But Worcestershire still needed 14 with two overs to go and could not breathe easily until Weston smashed the next ball from Watkin for another six.

Poor old Glamorgan have still to win a championship game. Yet on Abergavenny market day there was a big crowd sardined into this lovely ground, many of them irregular watchers rather than the defeat-weary faithful of Swansea and Cardiff. They saw 561 runs in the day and left exhilarated.

EVERYTHING STOPS FOR LUNCH ...
August 1988

This is how the worst ends ... not even with a whimper, actually, but amid a huge horse-laugh at the dottiness of cricket. At Lord's England finally did break their sequence of 18 Tests without a victory: but not on Saturday as they might; not on Monday as they hoped; nor even before lunch yesterday as they ought.

At one o'clock England were one run short of victory after Tim Robinson had failed to score off three successive deliveries. 'When the clock strikes one ... dum-de-dum ... everything stops for lunch.' And the Sri Lankan fielders were heading pavilionwards well before the umpires. Quite right: the sky was darkening; it might have rained. It did not. Forty minutes and four balls later England completed victory by seven wickets, a less emphatic margin than seemed probable on Thursday and Friday, but convincing enough.

The hiatus was extremely funny to everyone except Graham Gooch and John Emburey, who were anxious to be off playing elsewhere – no, not Bloemfontein – but in the county matches at The Oval and Hove. Before lunch they stood anxiously on the balcony looking at their watches. Robinson presumably believed there was time for one more over.

One small reform needed is the introduction of digital clocks to save arguments over at least one matter. A more logical fixture list is also needed. However, the clash between the last day of the last Test and the start of critical four-day championship games is scheduled to recur next year.

Even after the victory, the players still could not get away. The reporters released Gooch from the obligation of a post-match Press conference: he had spoken at length on Monday night and, anyway, some of us have backed Essex for the championship. Other people were less obliging. The presentation ceremony had to go ahead and since the litany for that includes the phrase 'Cornhill Insurance' repeated several times, it had to go on television, which could not happen for another five minutes, until *Neighbours* had concluded on BBC 1. That is the channel without advertising.

At eight minutes past two, Gooch finally jogged to his car, keys in one hand, thigh pad in the other. They used to say that when the raucous Tony Lock appealed at The Oval, someone was out at Lord's; but that was meant to be a joke not a precedent.

The chairman of selectors, Peter May, far from being at both grounds, was apparently at Scarborough where there is a festival game today between MCC and, bizarrely enough, Michael Parkinson's XI. Parkinson is presumably the successor to H. D. G. Leveson-Gower and the other worthies who used to pick these teams. It was Parkinson who, in the days before he joined the establishment, christened it the Marylebone Clodpoles' Club. No clodpole, May. He again left Micky Stewart to answer the difficult questions.

There was nothing further to be said on the political implications, if any, of Gooch's appointment. But Stewart admitted that one factor in making him captain[1] was that the selectors wanted him as a player. In other words, young man, if you want to be England captain do not play regular Tests, play hard to get instead. Stewart also admitted that the sacking of the original captain, Mike Gatting, who had led England to three one-day wins and a Test draw against West Indies, was a major cause of the failures that followed. 'It was the biggest blow we suffered,' he said. 'Gatting is a man who cares very much about the England side.'

[1] As captain of the touring party to India, which never left.

A REPUTATION TEETERING GLORIOUSLY ON THE BRINK
June 1989

We sometimes argue about the cricketer we would choose to bat for one's life (consensus answer: Don Bradman for your life, Geoff Boycott for his own). At Lord's yesterday David Gower came the nearest anyone is likely to get to that in reality: he was batting for his reputation.

The three and a half hours he was at the crease yesterday provided one of the most enthralling passages of play even an Ashes series has produced. Gower's negligent captaincy was largely responsible for putting England in this mess. His batting provided the one chance to get out of it.

This went beyond sporting drama; it was human drama. Gower's outward demeanour this game has been wonderfully casual: out in the sunshine all day Saturday, a few words *de haut en bas* to the press, then rushing off to the theatre for *Anything Goes* before a Sunday lie-in and the Wimbledon garden party. But Gower has always worn the mask of levity. Some perceptive observers thought that on Saturday he was actually close to breaking point and that the Burlington Bertie act was covering up something like despair. Kim Hughes resigned in tears in less of a mess than this. There is a powerful analogy, too, with the Allan Border of 1986–87, who approached the first Test with a supposedly fierce pace attack that was blown away on the first morning of the series. Border's morale was blown away with it.

Now the roles are reversed. Border's apparently relaxing few months with Essex now look like one of the most audacious spying expeditions since the Nazis got their man in Turkey employed as the British ambassador's valet. He watched, he listened, he learned. England have been boneless and brainless and the world knows it.

There was only one way out for Gower, and he did it immaculately. No one ever imagined that he would lead England to the Ashes with his own masterplan. It was reasonable to suppose that he would lead the team from the front, as he did in 1985, and show some extra maturity. And here at last was an innings which suggested that somehow, somewhere England will stand up and start fighting properly.

Gower was never secure. It was like watching a man inch his way along a parapet. Every now and again he would wobble and play an uppish one and there would be the queasy feeling that he was about to fall off. Then he would produce a stroke of purest essence: an off-drive or a little flick past point. His eye may not be as quick as it was. Heaven knows what goes on in his head. But Gower still brings a unique and instinctive artistry to his batting. It needs to be appreciated and cherished and encouraged to flourish as long as possible, because we may not look on its like again. England's next generation promises to be brimfull of heavy-bat thumpers like Robin Smith.

Gower's performance at his Saturday press conference was only slightly less remarkable. England captains have used these occasions to get their own back on their critics before now: there was Brearley's grand rant after the Headingley Test of 1981; Bob Willis' monosyllables-and-grunts-only show at Lord's in 1983; and Gower's own threatened walk-out at Madras in 1985. But these came in victory. Captains in defeat have usually known they need every friend they can get.

Gower's bizarre attitude merely rounded off one of the worst days any England captain has had: 'The world's gone mad today. And good's bad today. And black's white today. And day's night today ... Heaven knows, anything goes.' There is still no sign of an England strategy in this series, and everyone is bewildered. I reckon I could read the Queen's lips as she shook hands with Gower and said goodbye: 'And why didn't you bowl Foster from the Nursery End?'

2

PLAYING THE WHITE MAN

This is a short selection of reports from South Africa, starting with the first day of the rebel cricket tour, by the dirty dozen (later known as the South African Breweries English XI) in March 1982. I was the only English journalist also to cover the West Indian and Australian variations on this little divertissement. This was mainly because I planned a book on South African cricket, before eventually deciding that life really was too short.

Sportswriters usually either think South Africa is wonderful and uncritically accept Government-inspired hospitality, free trips and distortions; or they are righteously repelled and refuse to have anything to do with the place. I am unusual, in that I am both fascinated and revolted. It is a more complex country than some of its opponents allow: scenically beautiful, of course, but also sometimes touchingly old-fashioned and charming. Cricket brings that out. The atmosphere at a floodlit one-day game in Sydney now approaches the bestial; in Johannesburg it is festively innocent.

And yet everyone in South Africa is inevitably touched by the barbarism of its political system. Cricket has, quite obviously, become a tool of South Africa's opponents who are more interested in boycotts than sport. But the regime is involved too. The happy pictures of Englishmen coaching ghetto kids have become a propaganda tool. By dismantling an irrelevant piece of apartheid, the government is better able to shore up the rest of it. South Africa's cricket officials are able to protest to outsiders that they are wonderful liberal humanitarians fighting hard against the system. And yet they are part of that system. The rebel tours, we learned later, were funded by huge tax incentives to the companies who sponsored them.

I hope these pieces convey something of the flavour of the country without going too deeply over the old pro- and anti-boycott arguments. As well as cricket, they include stories on golf and soccer and what was almost certainly the first and last account in any British newspaper of the game of jukskei. One man's exclusive is another's total waste of time.

UNDER A STRANGE SOUTHERN SKY
March 1982

Pretoria: If there was ever a time when turning back was a plausible option, that time almost certainly ended at 11 o'clock Pretoria time yesterday morning when Graham Gooch and Geoff Boycott walked out together – as they have done so often under other skies and circumstances – to open the batting for something now being called the South African Breweries English XI. By the evening the players had still not seen the telex message sent by George Mann and Donald Carr, chairman and secretary of the Test and County Cricket Board, pleading with them to reconsider their decision to play in South Africa.

Gooch, as captain of the English team, held a Press conference in the ladies' toilet and changing-room at the Berea Stadium at close of play, when he insisted he would only answer questions about the cricket. Since the cricket on the first day of this extraordinary venture was rather dreary (Breweries English 152 for seven declared in four hours plus; South African under-25 XI 51 for one), this was not a great success. Asked if he would still be here in two or three weeks' time as planned, Gooch said doggedly: 'We'll be here at 10 o'clock tomorrow morning.'

All kinds of conflicting pressures are at work on the hearts and minds of the adjectival dozen. But Carr and Mann can only send telexes. Peter Cooke, the joint impresario and manager, was at Gooch's elbow. 'If they renege on their contracts, they could be sued under British law,' he said. And when Cooke is not with them, the players are talking and drinking with people who are wildly enthusiastic about a tour which they believe marks the end of their 12-year isolation from international cricket.

Indeed, the greatest threat to the tour's success yesterday probably came not from Lord's but from Boycott, who scored two runs in the first hour, 13 in 95 minutes in all, and must have made many spectators wonder if there was not something to be said for isolation. Around 3,000 people were there to watch, which is almost 3,000 more than Kerry Packer got on his first day of operations, and was particularly remarkable in Pretoria, the most Afrikaans and rugby-minded of major South African cities. Cricket here is a minority taste. Pretoria is also the whitest of the major cities, which may explain why the only blacks on the ground appeared to be employees.

The '13th man' mystery continued. Derek Randall, the latest to be touted, is in Perth, Australia, and said he was not the answer. The organisers have promised an announcement this afternoon and boasted that they had plenty of willing cricketers to choose from. My understanding is that they would have settled for Alvin Kallicharran, who is playing for Transvaal and thus already in disgrace back home in the West Indies, but the South African Cricket Union want it to be an Englishman so their 'Tests' can look like Tests.[1]

There was not a hotel room to be had in Pretoria though that was nothing to do with this match. The South Africa swimming championships are on and if no one else will play with you, such occasions are to be savoured. But the papers were full of the cricket with Fleet Street comment reported back and described as 'hysterical' even in the liberal *Rand Daily Mail*, which devoted eight chunky paragraphs to a pro-tour telephone call it received from one London cricket follower.

It was a glorious day – it is late summer south of the Equator – with temperatures in the high 70s and just a hint of possible showers in the late afternoon clouds. The Breweries, who have a virtual monopoly, did good business. After the initial excitement died down, it was like a particularly sunny and profitable Wednesday at Chesterfield or Abbeydale Park or any other of the nicer, leafier English grounds.

Before long, some people were turning away from Boycott and started to play with tennis balls amongst themselves. Chris Old, left out of the 12 by consensus, brought out drinks. Gooch batted quite aggressively for 33. Then the middle order collapsed to a blond fast-medium bowler from Western Province called Adrian Kuiper, who is regarded here as the find of the season. He bowls a little like Garth Le Roux and bats, so it is said, like Clive Rice. He finished with five for 22 off eight overs and, since it is only a two-day match, the English declared, a little sheepishly, more than an hour before the close. Gooch, when he had his way and talked cricket, moaned about the pitch. But it seemed flat and reasonable to me.

'Did you feel any undue pressure?' someone asked him. 'No, not on the cricket side.' 'What about on anything else?' 'I'm not answering about anything else.' The toilet windows were open and it was just possible to hear the lovely, half-forgotten sound of a steam locomotive chugging through Pretoria station. I had not imagined anything could make the scene more unreal.

[1] The eventual, anti-climactic solution was that the Warwickshire wicket-keeper Geoff Humpage joined the tour.

PAINFUL TRANSITION OF OMAR HENRY
March 1982

Cape Town: A 29-year-old coloured man called Omar Henry walked out to bat for Western Province against the rebellious English on the Newlands ground at Cape Town yesterday. Six years after the integration of South African cricket and a week into cricket's latest world war, no one gave him a second glance or registered more than the regulation amount of applause. There is nothing new in him being there. Non-whites have always been allowed onto the pitch to tend the grass or, before the war, lay down the matting wickets. Sir Pelham Warner wrote of how 'scores of Kaffirs' stretched the mats before each innings on the tour of 1898-99.

Henry, a batsman with a taste for occasional belligerence and a fastish slow left-arm bowler in the Underwood mould, is an established member of the Western Province side with a slim but definite chance of playing for South Africa before the so-called Test series is over. He is a modest and very pleasant man; after two years' club cricket in Glasgow he will be qualified to play for Scotland in the Benson and Hedges

Cup this year. His team-mates at Western Province called him Mac Henry; his former friends call him all kinds of other names, if they talk about him at all. Many, perhaps the majority, of the Cape Coloured community, have disowned him. 'I would not have him in the house,' said Hassan Howa, president of the (primarily) non-white South African Cricket Board.

Newlands is probably the world's loveliest cricket ground, filled with oak and plane trees with Table Mountain as a towering backdrop. The pitch and facilities are superb. Turfhall Park, five miles up the road, is where Henry (and indeed Basil D'Oliveira) used to play. It has four pitches, two of them the kind of mats on which Sir Pelham played and, by the looks of them, probably the same ones. The main square has a choice of two wickets, pitted or very pitted. They are used alternately. The out-field is hummocky and, after the long, arid Cape summer, bone dry. Across the park a sharp south-easter is raising a dust storm round a junior game.

Turfhall is used six days a week all the year round – for soccer, rugby and netball out of the cricket season. Coloured schoolchildren have to play on it because there is nowhere else; and though they try to schedule major league fixtures for other, slightly better grounds, some still have to be played here. Officials estimate that it would cost £40,000 to run the place properly; their basic income is £10,000. This year they could not afford fertiliser.

Henry is not a hero to the men of Turfhall. When the racial barriers in cricket were breached in 1976, he joined a club in the posh white liberal area of Green Point. He is said to have 'gone to the other side' in the terms mystics use to talk of the dead. If a Turfhall player went to any match at Newlands he would be ostracised, the more so for a game with the dirty dozen, a phrase they have adopted with relish. 'Henry can play with the whites,' said one. 'But he cannot live with them. His children cannot go to school with theirs and if he sets foot on Muizenberg Beach he will be arrested. Anyway, he wasn't even one of our best players.'

This is a point that Henry freely concedes and he admits that his transition has not been painless. He has been turned out of a steak house up the road from Newlands and a hotel in Port Elizabeth; on that occasion the whole team walked out with him. He is convinced that he will never be turned out again. 'I know some coloured people are against me. They can crucify me if they want to but I reckon I have the right to do what I want. Why must you say that because the country is wrong, cricket must suffer? What I am doing is one way of changing the country. And this tour has got to help the cricket situation in the whole world.'

Some non-whites either see things Henry's way or like their cricket well enough to go to Newlands anyway. In a community that is not even permitted to vote, one can only guess at the consensus, but the non-white attendances so far on the tour have not been impressive. Those who did go yesterday mostly went on the little train which runs from Cape Town to Newlands and Muizenberg, passing stations called Clovelly and Plumstead. The carriages are segregated. From the train in the morning there was a clear view of a huge brush fire that is raging across part of Table Mountain. The fires to come can be seen better from Turfhall.

DIVIDING PIN LINKS THE UNTROUBLED AND UNWANTED
March 1982

Pietersburg: In the deep north of South Africa, near the border with what people are reluctantly learning to call Zimbabwe, the local white sportsmen remain untroubled by the UN blacklist and boycott.

This is because their sport is so rustic, tribal and obscure that they can be fairly sure South Africa's opponents have never heard of it. Yet it is part of the history and soul of the Afrikaaners who rule the country. The sport is a vigorous version of bowls called jukskei. On Saturday they were holding one of the main provincial competitions, the Holiday Inns Tournament, at a place called Pietersburg, which sounds pre-revolutionary and may well be.

However, current political developments are of a different nature. This is the centre of the fight against the Prime Minister's talk of reform. Pietersburg is just north of Waterberg, constituency of the Right-wing Nationalist rebel Andries Treurnicht – Dr No. The local MP, Willie Snyman, supports him. The average jukskei player is slightly to the Right of the sabre-tooth tiger.

But oddly, politics, which dominates the conversation of so many people in South Africa, hardly cropped up all day. The average English mother-tongued urban South African will, within five minutes of meeting you, demand to know what you think of the state of his country, get ratty if he does not like the answer and then say petulantly that it is nothing to do with him, it is those rotten backwoods Afrikaaners.

The backwoods Afrikaaners who play jukskei did not ask my politics; they were happy enough with their own not to care. Instead they told me how the honey bee lurked among the aloes and how they used to harvest the mealie cobs in the good old days. It was delightful. During the speeches, *The Guardian* was placed on the platform and, probably for the first time in South African history, applauded. I expected to be sussed any minute and kicked out; instead they were wonderfully hospitable and charmed that I was interested in their sport.

Jukskei players lob a hefty piece of rubber, shaped like a bottle or a Mini's exhaust pipe, at a stake placed in a sand pit 50 feet away. Mostly, they aim to hit the stake, for which they get three points; there is one for a near miss. The cunning bit is that they have to finish on exactly 23 points. The game was played to similar rules on the Great Trek north in 1838 when, at dusk, the young Boers would chuck the dividing pin from an ox-yoke at a stick in the ground. There were no other sporting implements available. But the game fell away with the ox wagon and was kept alive only on the beaches until, a century later, the Afrikaaners reasserted themselves and revived their culture and their sport.

There are 10,000 registered players and it is taught in Afrikaans schools. They even have internationals – with the United States, whose horseshoe throwers have been introduced to the game. The Americans are sending a team to the national championships next month, provided someone from the UN does not read this and stop them.

The sport is integrated in the traditional Afrikaaner way: the whites play the game and a black prepares the barbecue. No black has ever applied to do anything else. I felt obliged to mention this to George Hambidge, vice-president of the jukskei board, and one of the few people of English descent to take up the game. He began what could be the national anthem: 'You don't understand how it is with the blacks in this country. When you have been here just a little longer ...' I dropped the subject and joined the barbecue.

THE MONEY-GO-ROUND AT BUTLINS IN THE BUSH
December 1983

Sun City: Without difficulty or worry Severiano Ballesteros yesterday won the million-dollar Sun City Tournament and its attendant £200,000 first prize. It was easily the biggest pay-day of his career and four times what he will get should he win something as trivial as the Open next year.[1] It is also about one thousand times the per capita national income of the tournament's bizarre host nation, Bophuthatswana (hereinafter, in accordance with local usage, known as Bop). That last figure, anyway, is a record.

Ballesteros was never remotely threatened after he had shrugged off Nick Faldo halfway through the third round on Saturday. He hit long and straight and completing his fourth successive sub-par round, a 68, he stretched his overnight lead of three strokes to five. He finished on 274, 14 under par, ahead of Faldo, David Graham and Fuzzy Zoeller, who charged from the rear end of the 10-man field with a last round of 65, a tournament record.

Faldo was unfortunate, if that is the word at this income level. On Saturday his putts would not go in; yesterday he missed his saving putt on the 18th to lose outright second place. Even more tantalisingly his tee-shot flirted with the hole at the par-three 16th, where there was a spot prize of £150,000 for a hole in one. The poor man had to settle for an Audi for the nearest miss and £70,000 for joint second.

The money, as negotiated with reference to tax breaks between Sol Kerzner, who runs Sun City, and the president of Bop, Lucas Mangope, boggles even the golfers' minds; and the mentality seems to be getting through to the locals. Last week an unemployed miner, Tadina Gora, reportedly walked 20 miles from his shack with his last £30, put it all in a slot machine and, with three coins remaining, hit a £20,000 jackpot. It could never happen in South Africa proper because, even if the machines were allowed in, Gora would not be.

This is not the normal stern pattern of African development either but Bop, in seven separate bits with South Africa in between, is not a normal African state. To its credit, as it celebrates six years of what passes for independence, it is not even close to the norm of South African homelands since Mangope is not a thug.

The biggest jackpot of all, however, goes to Kerzner. He is married to a former Miss World, Anneleine Kriel, and now controls all the gambling dens in the South African microstates. Sun City, within three hours' drive of Johannesburg, is by far the most important. (Local joke: if Sol and Anneleine get divorced, who gets custody of Mangope?)

Kerzner was flying over this desolate and scrubby valley and said something like: 'Let there be a 600-bed hotel complex with casino, 8,000-seat indoor arena, golf course, roller disco and appropriate fast food outlets.' And lo, it came to pass: Butlins-in-the-Bush. They drive up from Johannesburg in their thousands and the unforgettable smell of the African night is overpowered by hamburger and chips.

If much of Sun City is downmarket Kerzner can still show golfers, the celebrities and the high rollers a very good time. Liberace and Dickie Henderson were on at the pre-tournament dinner, if you like that sort of thing, and no one was too distraught about the threat of being blacklisted and never again being able to play the Ougadougou Hippodrome or the Equatorial Guinea Open.

Kerzner generally gets who he wants as well. Only Tom Watson of the world's leading golfers has eluded him. This time, when the black American, Calvin Peete, withdrew – officially through back trouble, though there was a persistent rumour that the anti-apartheid people had got to him – Kerzner sent for and got Larry Nelson even though Gary Player, who designed the course, was on the spot and feeling miffed at being left out. There is still money to burn. Next year Kerzner is likely to dump the celebrity element of the early part of the tournament and instead bring in some of the leading women golfers or sentimental favourites. That might be good news for Player.

The course is beautifully kept and, though very long, is not too stiff by the highest standards. This is a subsidiary reason for the event's attractiveness. Everyone in this field broke par over the 72 holes. Kerzner is also talking about a sister event in the Transkei to go with it – a sort of tour of Erewhon.

Some of the money is sluiced through into the local economy. Without Sun City around everyone, at least those who can stay off the slot machines, would be worse off, which will be a reassuring thought for Ballesteros to take home with his loot, if he cares to think of it.

Touring golf – airport to hotel, the golf course and back – is inevitably removed from its surroundings. But so far as is known there are no forced resettlement camps in the immediate vicinity of Royal St Georges, Sandwich (like the one near here for people who have been under the delusion that they were South Africans) nor villages where most of the children have square heads due to vitamin D deficiency. It would be reassuring if one sportsman, just one, showed signs of contemplating the strange juxtaposition of things at Sun City and wondering if it was not a question so much of whether sport should be exempt from politics as of whether it should be exempt from any contact with reality at all.

[1] Which he did.

REBELS WITH A NEW CAUSE
December 1983

Johannesburg: Anyone who has attended, or even read about, floodlit cricket in Sydney will be aware of the special atmosphere – the heightened partisanship, the whiff of cordite even – that attends one of these strange occasions, probably Kerry Packer's second most important bequest to the game. This week the South Africans, who have replaced Packer as the scourge of the international cricket establishment, also staged a floodlit international. It was as tensely contested as any cricket match can be: Lawrence Rowe's rebel West Indians beating the South African national team by two wickets with four balls remaining at 11.21 p.m., which is hereby offered as the world lateness record.

The Wanderers ground was packed with 30,000 people. The players were thoroughly bad-tempered. Though the crowd did not know it, and the Press had the merest inkling, the West Indians were squabbling about money (that is Packer's most significant bequest) and had almost refused to play. The row was only settled at 4 a.m. on Friday after talks through the night to agree on a new sponsorship deal.

Nonetheless it was clear during the game that something was up. There were several moments of animosity involving players and umpires, most obviously when the South African captain Peter Kirsten kicked a stump away after the West Indians had tried to run him out. In Sydney, the effects would have been inescapable: beer cans and fists flying; armed police storming up the Hill to throw people out. South Africa is not a placid country. Last weekend 31 people died violently in Soweto and it only rated three paragraphs in the *Rand Daily Mail*. There is no shortage of armed policemen. Yet at The Wanderers, there was no need of them. The South Africans, it should be noted, were wearing lurid yellow, the West Indians would have been in maroon had they not stuck to traditional white as part of their protest, the stumps were painted Day-glo orange and the umpires were wearing nylon jackets.

The players' argument is over now. The West Indians, who want to negotiate their own sponsorship deal, have been placated by the local Yellow Pages people, who are putting

£140,000 into the five remaining one-day matches. Their 17 players have come out of this affair looking greedier than ever. It is improbable that this will materially affect the good feeling towards them from the white public. When dusk fell at the match and the floodlights were switched on, bathing the gum trees in a weird creamy light, the whiff was not of cordite but of sausages, wafting up from dozens of barbecues set up by the practice ground.

Round the stands, the crowd oohed and aahed and applauded the teams just about equally. They seemed quite uncertain which side to support, their own country or their new buddies from the West Indies, who have come to see a poor lonely nation whose pals from the old days no longer come to call. The result apparently displeased no one. In a way, it was very pleasant – better than Sydney or a Somerset Sunday match. But it was also very odd. As a side-effect of isolation, the South Africans have missed out on most of the trouble inside cricket grounds that bugs everyone else. At Cape Town the other week the kids swarmed on with autograph books during a drinks break and no one minded. The Lord's announcer would have gone berserk.

But the best cricket is characterised, if not by the hatred that the Australians whip up as a marketing gimmick, then at least by a spirit of amiable loathing. South African crowds, whether they are playing rebel or official teams in the years to come, will not bring themselves to wish real ill-will on the West Indians, not in our lifetime.

The crowd, as has always been the case in Johannesburg, was almost exclusively white. This is partly a reflection of the traditional African preference for soccer. But The Wanderers, though the club is now open to people of any race, is more than any other cricket ground a place for the rich. It is sited, beautifully, in the midst of the northern suburbs five miles out of town with very poor public transport. It is hard to reach for the poor whites living just south of the city centre, never mind the people of Soweto 20 miles away.

John Passmore, the kindly Cape Town gent who organises special cricket weeks for Africans, says that there has been greater interest since the arrival of the West Indians. But there are still only three cricket clubs for the million inhabitants of

Soweto and *The Sowetan* newspaper still fills its sports page with endless chit-chat about soccer (Cape Town Spurs want Crooks and Brooking, by the way), nothing about cricket.

Even the whites will not be diverted by these West Indians forever. Most close observers are now convinced that this will be the last rebel tour for some time. Joe Pamensky, president of the South African Cricket Union, told me there will be no more tours this season and that he is personally recommending to his committee that there should be none next.

As we know, this is not in itself a reliable guide. Pamensky told me: 'If there was a tour, I wouldn't tell you. But there isn't.'[1] He then went on to say why there should not be one: the need to stop the restlessness among South Africa's domestic sponsors, who are tired of having their products overshadowed; the fact that South Africa has had four tours in 18 months, and that the market has been saturated; and the growing tendency of cricketers round the world to have a very high idea of their value indeed. Pamensky specifically ruled out the idea of a World XI of available players – 'Absolutely not. People don't come and watch games like that.' My impression is that only something sensational – the sudden availability of the full Australian team, say – would change his mind.

But Pamensky is generally one jump ahead, even when changing down a gear. In the midst of the World Cup, when we were all hysterically speculating about the game's best-known names and sums with a lot of noughts on the end, he was quietly down at East Molesey watching Monte Lynch in a Sunday league match. No doubt he is cooking up something now. If his annual visit to the ICC in 1984 can be conducted in a calmer atmosphere, it might bring the lingering pro-South African sentiment at Lord's back to the surface. And the South Africans do want to be liked, they do want to rejoin the fold, they do not want to spend the rest of their lives having 4 a.m. meetings with Lawrence Rowe.

So what hope is there for them? In the immediate future, none whatever. Internally the rival, black-led South African Cricket Board will not merge with Pamensky's group and if they did would be disowned by their parent body SACOS, and another splinter cricket group would emerge. Furthermore,

Gerrit Viljoen, the minister in charge of sport, told the absurd expenses-paid jamboree for rugby writers in the summer that there could be no normal competition between the races at school level. And for the UN and the Third World that would have to be a starting point.

[1] And there wasn't – for two years.

A BLACK FLOWERING IN THE WHITE STREETS
December 1985
BLOEMFONTEIN CELTIC 2   AFRICAN WANDERERS 1

Johannesburg: The biggest footballing surprise on Saturday almost came not at Anfield or Old Trafford but, believe it or not, at Ellis Park, Johannesburg, where Bloemfontein Celtic, red hot favourites for the South African Cup, were held until the 27th minute of extra time by African Wanderers, a Durban team with no coach and apparently no hope.

Celtic, the only full-time professionals in the country, won all right in the end, when a youngster called Ismael Mokitlane finished off a lone run with a narrow angled shot between keeper and post. But it was an epoch-making final anyway, the product of a South Africa a long, long way from rebel cricket tours.

For a start, this was the first final since the new National Soccer League (NSL) broke away from several other confusing sets of initials. It sounds like another bout of South African politics. But the plain truth is that the big clubs split from the rest to get a bigger slice of the financial action.

It was also the first final not to include any of the major Soweto clubs. The organisers panicked at this and almost switched the game to Bloemfontein, where soccer has recently started out-drawing rugby. But Wembley is Wembley, special trains were laid on from Bloemfontein and Durban, and 60,000 turned up, of whom well over 59,000 were black, the main exceptions being two Wanderers players, two linesmen, and a family sitting near me who ostentatiously remained seated when the black anthem, Sikelele, was sung rather than the official white version.

Bloemfontein is a highly unlikely soccer city, being more famous for rugger, religion and racism. Twenty years ago blacks were actually banned from watching the city's soccer team, never mind playing for it, and only this week it emerged that black traffic cops there are forbidden, under local regulations, to book white motorists. The rebuilt Ellis Park was supposed to be a temple to that South Africa. It was the product of the Transvaal Rugby Union and would probably have been a *folie de grandeur* even if times and the boycott had not got tough. A bank had to take it over.

Last week, there was a novelty golf tournament with greens and bunkers on the pitch while Gary Player and company teed off from high in the stands. I was terrified that someone would forget where he was and walk forward off the tee.

The pitch was still discoloured from this malarky, but no one seemed bothered. Six hours of hoopla were laid on before the match with rock groups and sky divers and the cup arriving by helicopter and Sir Stanley Matthews ceremonially kicking off.

The football struggled to match this, except when someone got injured and half a dozen St John's ambulance people, including a 15-stone lady at full waddle, rushed on to help the trainer. Both teams passed with great elegance, but often to each other. There was much over-ambition – overhead scissor kicks and the like. The moves that worked, worked handsomely but an average Third Division chopper would probably have caused mayhem.

No one expected too much of Wanderers. They are struggling against relegation, the coach Allan Varner resigned last month, and it is rumoured that they have only been training once a week. But they got here by killing giants like Kaiser Chiefs of Soweto, winners four times since 1979, and they hung on gamely after Celtic had gone ahead in the third minute.

They equalised just before half time, and could easily have snatched it. But Celtic, with pros from Malawi and Mozambique and a coach, Dave Roberts, who was (at least

124

briefly) with Liverpool reserves, were much fitter. As time
went on their dominance increased. The crowd reacted to the
winning goal with what seemed like acceptable jubilation/
despair to the eyes jaundiced by soccer in darkest England,
though the Celtic manager Petrus Molemela, in flowing green
robes, fell over everyone in rage.

They say it would have been different and far more violent
had the local clubs been involved. Maybe. But I walked away
among the 60,000 with far less trepidation than I have at
some cup ties I could mention. The white Sunday papers
yesterday gave the game slightly less space and prominence
than the English soccer news. Almost beneath their notice,
one begins to sense a new South Africa, pushing through to
daylight like spring growth after the long, white winter.

FLOODLIGHTS ON THE REBELS
December 1985

Johannesburg: It was a bad day for Australia on Wednesday:
beaten by New Zealand in the Perth Test; Kim Hughes' team
of alternatives beaten by Transvaal in the day-nighter in
Johannesburg; out of the soccer World Cup to Scotland.
Nothing directly to do with England but you know how it is. I
could not resist a dig. 'Oh come on,' said an Australian
journalist, 'we've still got the world barefoot water ski
champion.'

I believe they have, too. And perhaps even now the South
Africans are plotting a multi-million rand barefoot water
skiing tour. But, momentarily anyway, the unofficial
Australians are looking no better than the official version.
They have now lost one-day games twice running to
provincial teams and there is growing unease about their
prospects in the forthcoming international series. In one
sense, this was no disgrace. They were on the receiving end of
a remarkable blitz from the great Graham Pollock; and
Transvaal, anyway, are probably the strongest sub-
international team in the world. The South African XI, when

it is chosen, is likely to include seven of their players, the captain Rice, Pollock, the openers Cook and Fotheringham, the left-arm spinner Kourie, the wicket-keeper Jennings and the opening bowler Hugh Page, a rather broader version of our own Foster. They will probably be joined by four familiar county cricketers: Kirsten, McEwan, Le Roux and Jefferies.

Although Transvaal would doubtless dispatch Essex or Middlesex, the national side would, I think, be easy meat for Gower's England at present. Hughes' Australians, heavily dependent on their captain's batting and a collection of decidedly injury-prone fast bowlers, should be a different matter. That would be bad news for the South African administrators. They are committed to another tour next winter, probably with five five-day quasi-Test matches. It is vital that the opposition retains some credibility and appeal. But already several of the Australians have some fitness troubles. If they have to send for replacements they cannot, under the truce with the Australian board, poach any more of the leading players; the probable stand-ins are the batsman Rick Darling and the seamer Ian Callen, neither of them world beaters.

But the progenitors of these tours, Joe Pamensky and Ali Bacher, have been lucky as well as skilful in recent years. And so far people appear anxious to watch the Australians. The Wanderers ground was full on Wednesday night with 29,000, more than an entire Test seems to manage in Australia these days, and the game had the special atmosphere which seems unique to South African one-day cricket. In a superficial way the South Africans have out-Packered Packer. The Australians were dressed in a particularly vile shade of canary, and in the field wore every kind of cricketing headgear with the sole exception, sadly, of the traditional baggy cap. The stumps were a livid orange, and the umpires, heaven help us, wore blue tracksuits. And it used to be such a beautiful game.

But then, as the floodlights came on during the supper break, hundreds of people rushed onto the field, as ever in South Africa, with bats and tennis balls and frisbees, and no one trying to be a killjoy about it. At that moment, too, came one of those sudden Highveld downpours that arrives, does its worst, and then vanishes. Most of the ball players stayed on through the rain, and a few stripped off their drenched shirts and began sliding around on the tarpaulins covering the pitch. The locals chuckled. 'Oh yes,' said someone, 'there are some real crazies here. I bet we have a streaker before the evening's out.'

They didn't. One lad ran on to congratulate the Australian, Steve Smith, for his 93, and was hauled away by a steward for a lecture before being allowed back to his seat. Otherwise, the crowd remained on their uncomfortable wooden benches enjoying what ultimately became a rather dull game. Except at the entrance, I never saw a policeman.

The crowd was as near to all-white as you could get in any country south of Iceland without actually barring the gate to blacks. This is partly sporting taste, partly geography. The Wanderers ground is in the heart of the amazingly-affluent northern suburbs, where public transport is a rumour and the blacks are second-bottom of the social scale, some way ahead of the car-less.

The behaviour was a reflection of the extraordinary homogeneity and restraint South Africa can exhibit when there are no blacks around to be dealt with. I would guess most of the spectators went to the ring of local schools which produces the cricketers: all of them, state and private, retaining the ethos of English public schools 20 and more years ago. In the same way the Transvaal army held up the Empire in the Boer War, although its commanders were unsure from one day to the next which of their soldiers would pitch up and which would push off home to the farm. White discipline is one of the regime's most formidable hidden assets.

The crowd was not quite the largest of the week in these parts. Forty thousand had gathered the previous day in the township of Mamelodi to hear Winnie Mandela talk of vengeance at a mass funeral of blacks killed in the unrest. The police kept a low profile there too, though for different reasons. Except for the odd journalist, it seems most improbable that anyone was present at both events or knew anything, beyond the haziest outline, of the other.

At The Wanderers, when the supper-time rain eased off,

smoke canisters were lit as part of a sky diving display. That is the nearest Kim Hughes and Co. are likely to get to tear gas as they continue their love affair with the bright, shining, hospitable face of this country. Hidden away is a different South Africa, which the cricketers believe exists in the imagination of foreign journalists. Good care is being taken to ensure that they never see it, hear about it, or think of it.

A CENTURION OUT IN THE COLD
December 1985

Johannesburg: The other day, on the Jan Smuts ground in East London, Graeme Pollock, one of the greatest batsmen of our era, scored 113 for Transvaal against Border, his 61st century, and so passed 20,000 runs in his career. The innings, as ever with Pollock, was a bit special. The statistic, however, seems commonplace: after all, Dennis Amiss has passed 40,000 and Boycott is grinding on towards infinity.

Yet, to English eyes, it seems most remarkable that Pollock should now be playing at all. He is the last South African Test cricketer in regular business. Yet in a game where all the other great cricketers are playing each other into a stupor, it is as though Pollock had been killed in the trenches. He has been a world class batsman for a quarter of a century, yet he has not played in England, except for the odd charity match, since the Rest of the World series in 1970. The Australians hardly know who he is: even Packer had to pay him off and send him home, because the Jamaican government insisted their players could only consort with South Africans who had played at least six weeks of county cricket.

And, indeed, age has not withered him, nor the years condemned. Pollock is still, at almost 42, disgustingly close to the South African ideal: the blonde, all-purpose, unsullied sporting hero. Had he played more cricket, he would look much more haggard.

As it is, he keeps retiring. He was on the verge of giving up

128

in 1977, but a business move to Johannesburg took him away from ramshackle Eastern Province, where he carried the team, to highly professional Transvaal. He was going to pack in last year; then the Australian tour was announced, and he couldn't miss the Aussies, could he?

This season is definitely his last, he told me. But then, he reflected, the Aussies are back in South Africa next year ... and there was a decided flicker of interest when I mentioned the projected MCC bicentenary match in 1987. He still enjoys cricket. And he is still South Africa's best batsman. The eyes and the reflexes are not what they were and Hartley Alleyne gave him a fearful clonk on the head two years back, which would never have happened in the old days. Now he stands with his helmet clamped on and his feet so wide apart that he could hardly play an authentic back-foot shot if he wanted to. It is not necessary: if the ball is short he just rocks a little and pulls or cuts; if it is overpitched he drives with his three-pound lump of Fearnley's finest, and the ball is past the boundary.

To the South Africans, his status is close to godlike. None of the umpires dared give him out lbw until the Englishman Barrie Meyer came along a few years ago. ('You've started something,' he grumbled to Meyer some weeks after this epoch-making event. 'I've had five lbws in the past six innings, and only one of them was out.') And he had been content to stay in the laager.

He has toyed with county cricket at least four times: Nottinghamshire wanted him when his great mate, Sobers, was in charge; Somerset offered him the captaincy in 1969, but they were such a bad side then that he shied away; Leicestershire had a nibble; and not long ago Kent had a try, and he might have accepted if they could have offered a one-year contract rather than two. But he likes Jo'burg and his wife and his kids (son Anthony is supposed to be a left-hand natural just like his dad) and his winter golf and his job on the board of an industrial clothing firm, where he nails the orders before letting the customers harangue him about what Transvaal are doing wrong. He is not a poor man.

And since he has played 23 Tests with an average second

only to Bradman, the boycott has not gnawed at him the way it has with other South Africans. He has proved himself.

Pollock's politics remain close to the cricketing consensus. 'The whole South African political thing needed shaking up; and I must say thank goodness tours were cancelled. But it's become a matter of one-man, one-vote and that's totally unfair. It's an unreasonable demand at this stage. The world is just stringing us along. South Africa's been part of world cricket for so many years and our President can't even go into Lord's. I think that's diabolical. Rebel tours were the only route and they have had the desired effect; good players have come to South Africa, and if they have disrupted world cricket, maybe that's a good thing.'

And he remains an optimist. He believes the sports boycott means nothing now; the crucial pressure is political and economic; the government is going to have to announce a real reform package soon. 'There are these possibilities. I think things could happen, Test cricket even, surprisingly soon. A lot of countries really do want to play with us.' England v South Africa for real, with Pollock? 'Oh, no, it won't happen that soon. I'd just love to watch it.' But it's nice being with an optimist; it rubs off, if only temporarily. And whatever you think of the boycott, you have to say that a Test match, against South Africa or Azania, complete with Pollock, with no one feeling the need to cavil or demonstrate, would be the one happy, sporting end of the whole wretched business.

3

THE WONDERFUL AND
THE WEIRD

This is where the cricket finishes, and the dilettantism really begins. For my first year on *The Guardian* I went to soccer matches on Saturday afternoons, as I had done throughout my youth. Increasingly, however, I became disillusioned not so much with the sport, but with the ambience and the people who ran it, most of whom seemed thoroughly obnoxious.

Since the paper had no shortage of reporters who took a different view, I spent two winters – before starting my years of cricket touring – as the Minority and Miscellaneous Sports correspondent which meant, among other things, that I was expected to field the call whenever a loony rang the office. It was agreed that I would cover everything from those sports not quite important enough to warrant a correspondent of their own like, say, netball, to, well, tiddlywinks. Next morning, a Press release announcing the National Tiddlywinks championship arrived on the sports editor's desk and I was dispatched to report the occasion. The telephonist to whom I dictated my report had never heard of me and by the time I got to the third paragraph she left the phone to report this hoaxer to her superior.

It was a very pleasant couple of years. There were no competing journalists at the Fen skating or the underwater hockey; no self-important directors; no managers dispensing vacuous half-truths; just ordinary (well, occasionally slightly touched) folk doing what they enjoyed and nearly always gratified that someone should take an interest. Even when I wrote about cock-fighting in Martinique some years later, the people were at least pleased to see me.

This section mixes the conventional and the *outré*; my enthusiasms, like horseracing and baseball, mixed in with those sports which were, well, jolly interesting to see the once. It includes a few reports from the Seoul Olympics, one of the most fascinating experiences of my journalistic career and probably the major sporting event of the 1980s. At the end, there is a return to football and, for me, several reminders why I stayed away from it.

I still cherish the hope that I will have the health, energy and ability to report the sport of the 1990s and beyond. I still love it and, on the good days, can hardly believe that anyone is willing to pay me to write about it. I don't think cricket or any sport is the *only* thing worth caring or writing about. But as long as people care, then sport matters.

BASH STREET MEETS THE EDWARDIANS

April 1980

LEICESTER 1   CHELSEA 0

It was probably a little like this in the spring of 1907, another year when Leicester and Chelsea were both around the top of the Second Division; the sun on the new-mown turf, the clean-cut young players trying their honest, sporting best, the fouls committed only *in extremis* and then with apologies afterwards, the custodians hurling themselves fearlessly at the leather – the whole Corinthian bit.

Unfortunately, the analogy breaks down when you leave the playing area. The match was held up for three minutes because a number of young men with close-cropped hair and vacant expressions took time off from giving Nazi salutes, escaped into a zone reserved for normal human beings and began fighting. Several hundred spectators, many of them unaccompanied children, had to climb or be lifted to safety.

From the first can of warm lager in the morning to the last slammed train door at night, 39 people – 29 of them from London – were arrested and charged and 50 were taken to hospital. The only remotely novel part of all this was that, after the match, some yobs clambered over the spiked railings guarding the pitch; this could be good news for anyone who favours castration as a punishment for football hooligans.

Meanwhile, there was this first class game of football taking place, which Leicester should have wrapped up long before May headed in Edmunds' corner in the 65th minute. Both teams looked talented but unripe, which perhaps explains why they have been more accident-prone than promotion contenders ought to be. Leicester would certainly have been lost without the elderly skills of Kelly as a focal point.

Chelsea always wanted to attack but, except in the last few minutes, won insufficient possession to carry through their good intentions. Most of the hurling at the leather was done by their goalkeeper Borota. The tactics were engaging, nonetheless. Geoff Hurst, the Chelsea manager, said afterwards: 'We don't care what mistakes they make as long as they are positive about what they do.' He may even have meant it. Good luck to both teams; I hope they go up. Bad cess to their attendant loonies.

REBIRTH OF THE BLUES
May 1980
BIRMINGHAM CITY 3   NOTTS COUNTY 3

Birmingham City's point gave them promotion to the First Division along with Leicester but, if it's all right with you, we will take the euphoria as read. Anyway, Brummies do not stay cheerful long. An hour after the game, a man rang the local radio phone-in. 'Went down the Blues todye. Oy thowt the referee were diabolical.' Nothing else. The next caller sounded anguished. 'What'll happen next season?'

The junior supporters were more enthusiastic. Hundreds climbed onto the asbestos roof over the St Andrews executive boxes and jigged about, causing near-terror underneath until the police chased them off. Many of the dancers were completely bald, which suggested either a new fashion or an alopecia epidemic. They were too young to share the folk memory in which Birmingham always seemed to be about 19th in the First Division.

Perhaps it will work out this time. They have some good players like the goalkeeper Wealands, who made one outrageous save, and the lolloping but effective Bertschin up front. Jim Smith, the manager, intends to buy more. He needs to, because Gemmill occupies the same place on the field as Birmingham does on a motorway map of England, and even he is not getting younger.

Bertschin, Curbishley and Dillon scored for Birmingham; Mair, Christie and Kilcline for County, who came back from 2-0 and 3-2 down and employed a fascinating manoeuvre at free kicks – an attacking wall to block the defensive wall's view. This confused everyone, including County themselves, I dare say. When they attacked in the closing stages, there was almost as much panic in the home defence as in the executive boxes later.

DOUBLE TRIUMPH FOR THE WITHAM WINKER
November 1980

Just in case you missed the news flashes last night, Jonathan Mapley, a 33-year-old chartered accountant from Witham in Essex, is national tiddlywinks champion for the second year running.

It was a victory for British style and sang-froid. Mapley is renowned for pulling out of trouble with risky shots; his main rival in the field of 24 was the world champ, Dave Lockwood, an American who uses a digital clock-calculator, plays the percentage shots and remembers all his own statistics. Mapley will continue to enjoy the fame the title brings him. Last year someone who had seen their picture in the local paper recognised his wife at the butcher's.

'We did consider changing the name of tiddlywinks to make it sound less silly,' said Mapley. 'But then if we told people we had this great game called murdling, or whatever, they would look and say, "Oh, that's just like tiddlywinks," so what's the use?'

Most winkers (note the terminology) are pleasantly self-deprecating about their little eccentricity. They have to be, since the battle with their wives to arrange escape for the weekend is often fiercer than the battle in prospect.

But the techniques are highly sophisticated and the competition keen. Upset results are rare in tiddlywinks because experts like Mapley, Lockwood and Alan Dean, five times British champ, are such superior tacticians to everyone else.

The game was brought out of the nursery in the 1950s by an enterprising manufacturer and two Cambridge undergraduates who between them introduced the principle of the squop – the tiddlywinks equivalent of the snooker – suiting your winks on top of your opponent's to prevent him from potting. The two undergraduates gave up the sport, and the games firm, so it is believed, gave up the ghost, but their initiative lived on. The Americans took it up and became good at it. But it was the Oxford club which added the final twist, the double squop, an almost unstoppable tactic which relegated potting to a side issue and turned most games into a strategic pile-up, cerebral but unthrilling.

Most of the top players have mathematical jobs. Some flip regularly across the Atlantic, especially Lockwood, who is an economist for Pan Am. Earlier this year, Pam Knowles, a 28-year-old accountant from Manchester, surprised everyone by winning the American title. She was made redundant on her first day back, which rather spoiled things.

Mrs Knowles, the only woman to reach the final test, was down the field yesterday. Mapley was pressed hard by Cyril Edwards, a lecturer in medieval German, but eventually won through by crushing Lockwood in the final game in the students' union at Southampton University. He steered clear of the superstar stuff. 'It's nice to win again. It's a great game, a beautiful mixture of strategy and dexterity, luck and skill. Also, it's the one thing I'm really good at.'

A NIGHT IN TIERRA DEL COLDFIELD
December 1980

With the weather colder than a VATman's heart, nearly 400 people forwent mass-produced diversions on Saturday evening to run, trot and stagger round a snowy park in suburban Birmingham. They were competing in the British Night Orienteering championships, or at least they said they were. Night orienteering is a recent spin-off from the spikes, map and compass sport, which, less than 20 years after its arrival from Sweden, has collared the intellectual end of the jogging market. It is also the world's most complete non-spectator sport.

The participants, armed with cavers' lamps and thermal underwear, vanish through the trees into the blackness or, on this occasion, whiteness. They return an hour or so later, looking happy but knackered. Out of sight, they may be staging the annual *al fresco* dinner and dance of the Sutton

Coldfield Freemasons or performing Scandinavian sex-on-ice rituals. If you don't compete, you can't be sure.

Assuming they existed, the championships were held in Sutton Park, a venue with an inbuilt selection process. Getting there meant negotiating Spaghetti Junction, and only good orienteers stood a chance. By day, it is a friendly dog-walking heath and golf course, too straightforward for a major championship. By night, routine obstacles melt into menacing outlines and Sutton Coldfield can seem like Tierra del Fuego.

The orienteers are given specially-prepared maps and sent off at intervals; their only certainty is that the direct route will be impassable. No two runners will tackle a course the same way and even the experts are liable to hurtle off in the wrong direction from a checkpoint. However, they will quickly sort themselves out. Novices can disappear for hours.

'In daytime orienteering, you've got plenty of information to work from,' explains Roy Mason of the British Orienteering Federation. 'Your problem is to interpret it correctly. At night, you've got to get the information in the first place. You can't see a wood or an embankment unless you focus on it. It involves more concentration and it isn't for beginners.'

This lot were clearly the hard cases. Generally, they agreed that it was not that cold and that the course, though clever, was not too difficult. The main winners were Dave Kingham, who is doing a PhD at Cambridge in Field Evaporation from Transition Metal Surfaces and Kathy Crease, an undergraduate in urban studies at Sheffield. Both find orienteering a splendidly irrelevant hobby.

Last week, these two won the Midland night championships in Nottinghamshire and their repeat victories were unusual in a sport that often produces the unexpected. In the first race in England, a schoolboy with a flair for geography beat a field of Olympic athletes. That would not happen these days. Nonetheless, Kingham, not a world class runner, finished well ahead of the four-minute miler Glenn Grant. 'I'd say it was half running and half navigation. You've got to be able to run fast to win. On the other hand, you've got to know when to slow down.'

Even for the losers, it was jolly. The HQ, in a youth club, had the air of a cheerfully-shared hardship you get in a Lake District youth hostel on a Bank Holiday. The organisers asked, most courteously, if I could plug their sponsors, Batchelors. Rashly, I also agreed that next time, I would take part. Going home, I got lost.

HOLDS BARRED IN DUTCH TREAT
December 1980

Korfball is a kind of mixed netball, played either indoors or out. It is very big in Holland and North Belgium, very small in Britain. It is an extraordinary sport, carefully designed to cut out rowdyism, selfish play, star performers, over-specialisation and sexism. *The Guardian* woman's page should sponsor it.

Korfball is surely the only game specifically invented to be played by equal numbers of each sex (the only game except one, nudge, snigger). It was started by a Dutch teacher with advanced opinions, Nico Broekhuyzen, in 1902 for the pupils at his co-educational school in Amsterdam. It came here after the Second World War and has wobbled on uncertainly ever since. There are now just 1,500 players, all in South London and Kent.

The Dutch, who after all have taken to cricket, find our resistance to korfball baffling. They have more than 100,000 players – families spend their weekends down at the club – and they would like some decent opposition from us. So they are running a conversion campaign called Project England. They have hopes of bridgeheads in Alton, Hampshire, and Morpeth, Northumberland. Listen carefully and you can hear the echoes of bright-eyed Victorian missionaries sailing off to sell God to the Africans.

There was an important korfball occasion at the weekend, an international between the England under-21 side and a selection from Ghent in Belgium. It took place at Tolworth

Recreation Centre in Surrey, one of those sports halls with so many different coloured lines for different sports that the floor looks like one of Mondrian's dafter paintings. None of the lines, of course, was meant for korfball. Normally, korfball is played 12-a-side, six boys, six girls, but it is impossible to find a hall big enough. So to play indoors, they go down to eight-a-side, cut out the midfield and call it micro-korfball.

It was pleasant to watch, though everyone kept apologising and saying it was not a spectator sport. There were obviously skills involved apart from working out which lines were in use. Korfball baskets have no back board, which makes scoring tricky, and play goes on behind the goal so you can shoot from 360 degrees. Accurate, imaginative passing is crucial. In some ways, it reminded me of a Sunday afternoon in Bloemfontein. As soon as you think of something to do, you discover it is illegal. The boys have to mark the boys and the girls, the girls and, if the twain should meet, the result is almost certainly a free throw because all bodily contact is forbidden.

There is no running with the ball – a normal football – no kicking it, bouncing it, punching it or snatching it. Nor can you shoot if your opponent is in front of you and within an arm's length; you are expected to outwit him/her. Every two goals, attack and defence switch places so that no team can rely on specialist goalscorers or intercepters.

The standard of sportsmanship expected is astonishing. 'If the person marking you falls over,' said Peter Allen, the president of the British Korfball Association, 'you wait until they get up.' There was no opportunity to find out if he was pulling my leg because in the hour-long match, no one fell down at all except a toddler on the sidelines who had dropped her packet of crisps.

Korfball people say the game is not always so goody-goody. The Dutch are prone to argue with the referee and niggle with each other. There is immense importance in marking your opposite number and there is room for some furious staring matches. But touching, never. Well, hardly ever.

Last week, I encountered a doctor's theory that young judo players grow up better balanced than other people because they get regular body contact in the years between cuddles from Mum and regular sex. Heaven knows what the doc would make of korfball players. But the gap is probably shorter for them because the aprés-korfball provides such possibilities. There are a lot of korfball marriages.

The gallant Brits did well at Tolworth, fighting back from 5-1 down to lose only 11-10. The Dutch have hopes for us. The problems are finding pitches – Tooting and Clapham Commons are the current strongholds – and getting the sex ratio even. It is hard enough at parties, never mind sports events. As a game, it looks enjoyable and totally harmless. As a marriage bureau, it is probably more fun than a roller disco and more wholesome than the Young Conservatives.

ERIC'S ARROWS OF FORTUNE

January 1981

You may not be well up on homeopathy, though the Queen is said to be keen on it and Wally, my barber, certainly is. In homeopathy – I think I have this right – you cure an illness with tiny doses of substances that in larger quantities would actually cause it. It is the unique achievement of the BBC to discover the flip side of this principle and relate it to televised sports. They have found a game like darts, which viewers would chew up and spit out if shown a 10-minute segment on *Grandstand*, can become palatable and even addictive if served in massive daily helpings.

This week's Embassy World Professional championship on BBC2, the channel of Dr Bronowski and Lord Clark, was probably watched at peak by 10 million viewers. It has already spawned a national catchphrase (one-hun-dred-and-eight-ee), a record (same title) and a new, ethnic-sounding commentator called Sid, who read history at Cambridge, where they taught him to say things like: 'Stoke Newington's answer to Attila the Hun.'

The Attila in question is Eric Bristow, a 23-year-old former

140

furniture salesman who plays darts better than anybody else, a skill which a few years back would have won him regular pints and inscribed trophies. His gifts are suddenly marketable. On Saturday, at a Stoke-on-Trent nightclub called Jollees, he won £5,500 by throwing one last double four and beating John Lowe in the final. He may make £100,000 this year, helped by his gimmick of pretending to be less nice than he really is.

Bristow's win was historic, as Sid, the history expert, pointed out, because no one had ever before won the title twice. This is not entirely surprising since the competition only started in 1978. It was created with, for and by television and would not exist without it. It arose from the anti-homeopathic adventures of a senior producer, Nick Hunter, and a promoter, Mike Watterson, with the phenomenally successful World Snooker championships. The BBC hierarchy pressed Hunter to come up with another event where they could try the same format – building it up day by day, turning anonymous players into personalities, turning an otherwise routine event into a national obsession.

Hunter said darts, at which everyone fell about laughing: and then crying because, at first, they couldn't sort out the camera angles. Then someone suggested the split screen format, showing the players' faces and the board simultaneously. They were off and running. Not everyone was enthused, however, and Sid's commentary remains highly defensive. 'Who says darts isn't a sport?' he'll snarl occasionally.

Well, of course, it's a sport. It's not rigged and it's not a game of chance. (In 1908, the Leeds magistrates doubted this and a local landlord, charged with permitting a game of chance on licensed premises, had to earn his acquittal by beating the magistrates' clerk.) The question is whether it's watchable for hour after televised hour.

It certainly isn't watchable inside Jollees, a club as intimate as any 1,500-seat barn with purple lampshades on the Formica tables. Most of the paying customers could see only a vague impression of players and dartboard and had to follow the event on the marvellous electronic scoring contraption.

Bristow and Lowe were playing a game dependent on millimetres. Surely it would have been more fun to watch the two worst players in the world, spearing bystanders, wrecking the back wall, terrifying the barmaids.

Though they could not see it, they loved it. A lady from St John Ambulance said it was like a pop concert and someone was sure to faint. Two people kept cool: Attila, puffing away conspicuously on his freebie Embassys, little finger cocked, bum thrust in the air; Lowe, older, more orthodox, impassive. Both playing splendid darts. Bristow timed his victory so the Beeb could stay virtually on schedule. 'Yer wouldn't believe it,' cried Sid. 'They're standin' up, they're jumpin' they're rattlin' the glasses.' That was the audience, not the production team. Even the St John's ambulance lady was getting mildly hysterical.

What's next for your nightly blockbuster? Crib, perhaps, or dommies? No, though bowls and billiards are being talked about. Next at Jollees, they're billing 'The World's Foremost Hypnotist.' Give up, son, they're in a trance already.

A SCOOP FROM THE POOL
February 1981

This report comes to you from an inch or two below the surface of the deep end of the Carlton Forum swimming pool in Nottingham. This distinctly makeshift Press box is unlikely to be used again. For one thing, it has a deleterious effect on *Guardian*-issue biros and notebooks. For another, it has a deleterious effect on me.

However, there is no better way to report underwater hockey, a sport which – when you have quite finished sniggering – has spread since 1954 to more than 100 clubs in Britain and 20 countries worldwide. Here it is officially known, rather wittily, as octopush. It is much like any other form of hockey except that the sticks are only a foot long and spatulate; and there is the small complication of the water. It would like to be taken seriously.

Much of the limited newspaper and television coverage of octopush has been silly, often describing it as the ultimate non-spectator sport, which is incorrect, and resented. It is true that from the poolside a game looks like playtime in a school of sperm whales, especially when the 12 players surface and simultaneously blow out water through their snorkels. But from the edge of a glass-sided pool it would, I think, be worth watching. 'Better than football,' insisted Keith Johansen, the national competition's organiser. It is not the players' fault such facilities hardly exist in Britain.

The sport certainly started as a lark. Alan Blake, a skin diver in Southsea, dreamed it up as a way for the local subaqua branch to keep fit and interested out of season. If your hobby is exploring the seabed, the floor of the local chlorinorama can seem a little dull. Maybe half the 2,000 or so participants still play just to while away winter. Others have become keen enough to give up the ocean and concentrate on chasing the puck or 'squid'.

There are now embryonic world championships, a British team, sophisticated training programmes and tactical manoeuvres. The difficulty is putting theory into practice. The first problem down there is breathing – 30 seconds without air is most people's limit – the second finding the damp squid without getting shoved out of the way, the third successfully propelling it towards the goal or a team-mate. Someone may be shouting all kinds of advice or criticism but you won't hear a thing. It is a solitary sort of team game.

The Nottingham event was the second semi-final of the national championships. Six teams go through to next month's final, which the side from Harlow in Essex will probably win. Harlow won a big international competition in France two months back. It may well be the world capital of octopush, which would be appropriate; I have often thought that if forced to live there I would try and drown myself.

Octopush is a jolly sport – a test of swimming ability, endurance and skill – for people who are instinctively at home in the water. It is not for those of us who get hydrophobic reading the high tide tables for London Bridge. Ten minutes each way is standard and quite long enough to be knackering. There is a happy, boisterous atmosphere. Afterwards, the winners give the losers three cheers as on *Top Of The Form*. Women do play, but not much, and they are advised not to wear bikinis in mixed contests because, out of sight, the bottom half can mysteriously vanish.

There is an alternative game of underwater rugby known, with reason, as murderball. There is no sign of underwater cricket. Where are you, 'Kipper' Cowdrey? A number of other sporting events might sensibly be held under water including some Fourth Division football matches and a few annual general meetings. You will doubtless have your own nominations. In these cases, snorkels would not be provided.

THE SOUND WITHOUT THE FURY
March 1981

From the high perch in the Wembley Press box, it was just possible to discern far below in something like the seventh row of E block, the outline of a familiar and, in the circumstances, reassuring kind of figure. It was a man.

Behind, in front of and around him were 60,000 women, making a noise. At a guess, 50,000 of these were schoolgirls, 40,000 were wearing anoraks and blue jeans and 30,000 were waving flags bought £1 a time; which is pricy for a bit of cloth on a stick but cheap for a lethal weapon.

The annual women's hockey international at Wembley is one of the great occasions of sport, the more so this year because the Queen came for the first time, providing hockey with encouragement and Her Majesty with a novel experience. Nowhere else is the National Anthem sung quite so enthusiastically. During the match, she heard the unique Wembley screech, a crowd noise so piercing that they have to augment the whistle with a special buzzer sounding like a Trimphone. The players can only communicate by going over to each other and bellowing.

A century ago, when the leading girls' annual suggested

144

embroidery in chenille and French lacquerwork as the best recreations for young ladies, corsetted Oxford undergraduettes made the first feminine experiments with the boys' game of hockey – in secret, for fear of what people might say.

Now the roles are reversed. Men's hockey is still played widely and enthusiastically but there were 103 spectators at England's game with Poland the other night and that included the people in the restaurant. The women got more than Liverpool v Everton and as many as the whole Third and Fourth Divisions of the Football League put together.

It may be that some of the 60,000 had as they say, been volunteered. They came in charabancs, shepherded by teachers. The charas – 1,300 of them, someone said – stretched in a solid line all the way to Neasden, emblazoned with the resonant names of the coach firms of England – Hoyle's of Halifax, Tappin's of Wallingford, Kettlewell's of Retford, Grey-Green. Many had teasing, unofficial messages on the back windows, saying things like 'Boy Wanted.' In terms of supply and demand, they had come to the wrong place.

The players love it. Wales get their turn at Wembley every six years and their captain, Sheila Morrow, says there is nothing to touch it, though it is by no means an ideal hockey pitch. The grass is too long and the surface can be both spongy and bumpy. Val Robinson of England watched the League Cup final on television last week, just urging the teams to stay away from the penalty areas so as not to make them worse. Technically, they would all be happier on the smooth outfields of Lord's or The Oval. But, oh, that atmosphere.

The royal presence made everyone extra-nervy. My neighbour thought that some of the players spent more time watching the Queen at half time than listening to their respective rollickings – England for missing so many chances, Wales for not getting possession in the first place, a pattern much like a typical England-Wales soccer match.

The raging sou-wester obviously didn't help, buffeting the Royal Standard, the players' skirts and the players themselves. Somehow, the game was still highly skilled, good-natured – England and Wales know each other too well to get ratty – entertaining and exciting. When Jan Jurischka came on as substitute and immediately scored the winner, I nearly had a good shriek myself. No one else bothered to restrain themselves.

SCOTTISH SURFING SAFARI
September 1981

It would be mildly eccentric to hold the European championship of anything in Thurso, the northernmost town on the British mainland and last stop before Orkney, Shetland and oblivion. That turns to the downright bizarre when the sport concerned is surfing, which in most minds conjures up a picture of sun-kissed southern beaches where young men with deep tans, bleached-blond hair and sawn-off denims skive off work for ever. We will come back to that picture later. But the championship is on in Thurso and will be all the week, conditions permitting, which is a mighty big if in surfing.

The venue baffled most of the surfing community as much as it did me. I thought they must mean Truro. Most of the English team live in Cornwall and have made the sort of journey people normally make only when sponsored for charity or to antagonise the AA's get-you-home service. From here Britain seemed, if not great again, then at any rate big. At first everyone was agreeably surprised. The Pentland Firth is a new surfing frontier which turned out to be as good as anywhere in Europe. The waves that worry the fishermen delight the surfer, although it is perishing cold in and out of the water. The locals were as bewildered. There are said to be only three surfers in Thurso and the sport is unlikely to catch on even after the championship. Caithness people regard the sea as a business partner; a useful ally but one never wholly to be trusted and certainly not a playmate. Even for the surfers, the mix of wind – blowing from off the land to keep the waves alive – and swell has to be right. There are 16 potential sites near Thurso. Sunday was a dead loss at all of them.

The day was given over instead to meetings to which the French (gifted surfers, it is said, but difficult) sent a representative to protest about Britain's organisational grip and announce that his team were boycotting the event. Only the Spaniards have sent a full team from outside the British Isles. The competition is strong, nonetheless: between England and Wales, and even within the England team, where the ascendancy of Nigel Semmens – soon to become Britain's second-ever professional surfer – is being challenged by Paul Russell, an 18-year-old school-leaver from the unlikely surfing town of Leicester with a mad keen, cajoling dad, Eddie, who used to be a wing-half with Leicester City and Wolves.

By Monday, there is one usable site, at Sinclairs Bay near Wick. But that produced contemptible little ripples, learners' surf, unworthy of an expert's consideration. The heats were staged amid a lot of well-chilled moaning. Competitive surfers are normally expected to perform all kinds of stylish manoeuvres to impress the judges; here they were getting marks just for staying upright. 'It's not a surfing competition,' groaned one wetsuited loser. 'It's a swimming competition.'

But before nightfall, the waves began to pound at Thurso itself. The sense of joy returned. Semmens went in and began to taunt the water, sometimes playing a breaker as though it were a violin and he the bow, at other times dancing through and along it until surfer and wave became tired of each other and both fell flat with exhaustion. 'It's like skiing or skateboarding,' said Paul Russell, 'but with an extra dimension, as though you were on a moving ski-slope.' Yesterday, when the competition restarted, the surf had turned moody again. The wind was fierce all right but cut in straight off the sea, sending in more spume than wave.

There is no money in this championship at all. Semmens has no great hope of riches from being professional though he thinks sponsorship and a little prize money will keep him afloat. For the others, there is only the joy of being king of the beach, who, before surfing, used to be the chap that kicked sand in the face of the seven-stone weaklings.

With that, though, goes the drop-out image – surfers are widely assumed to score girls and dope with equal felicity and, worst of all, listen to Beach Boys' records. Of course it is unfair and the best surfers detest it; on the other hand, you cannot become Europe's champion surfer on the 8.17 to Holborn Viaduct. A lot of surfers have scorned more conventional opportunities to stay near the sea as lifeguards and surfboard makers; to that extent they are drop-outs, and good luck to them. 'I could live in Birmingham,' one said, 'but there aren't any waves there; there aren't any jobs either.'

DISCOVERED THE LOST SPORTING TRIBE
October 1981

The coelacanth is a sea creature which is acknowledged as a forebear of all our familiar little fishies. But until somebody caught one, it was regarded, by non-coelacanths anyway, as extinct. In the Scottish Highlands, there is a sporting equivalent, shinty, which lives and thrives in a very private way. And in the village of Newtonmore you can find the world's most famous shinty team. It is a funny kind of fame. Most Scots have heard of shinty. Some can even connect it with Newtonmore. But in the soft South (we are talking about Edinburgh and Glasgow) it is widely assumed that if the game still goes on, it is played only by massive bearded caber-tossers hooched up on quintuple Glen whathaveyous.

No one doubts that shinty is the mother or father of all stick and ball games – golf as well as hockey and ice hockey. But it is so steeped in myth and legend that you can see the mist rising. The old clansmen used shinty for battle practice; Newtonmore's home ground, 'The Eilan', has been a shinty pitch for centuries. The village is the traditional home of the Clan McPherson and a beautiful, bed and breakfasty place an hour south of Inverness. There are only 900 people there, but among the 900 are some of the greatest names from shinty's recent past: Johnny Campbell is the local builder,

Gaby Fraser runs a hotel, Jock Mackintosh makes the trains run on time.

The present team is the proudest yet. They won the Camanachd Cup, the chief honour, for the 25th time this year. Three of the side have nine Cup winners' medals. But there are fears for the future: the best players are ageing; the new A9 road is almost finished and the extra work that kept young men in the village may dry up; and other sports are creeping in – notably soccer, introduced, I was told blandly, by a bloody Englishman.

Newtonmore's match with the next village, Kingussie, makes the very mountains shake. Recently, however, they were away to Lovat, based at Kiltarlity, just north of Loch Ness. Kiltarlity is less obsessive about the sport. The soccer team share the pitch (which would never do at The Eilan), playing across it – a shinty pitch being half as big again. The goal is higher but narrower than in soccer and there are 12 players a side.

About 80 people turned up. The atmosphere was like a village soccer match, but a particularly tribal one. Passing by, you might think it was hockey, but a closer look would show that it was very uninhibited hockey. It is also a much more aerial game. The sticks are designed to loft the ball, like a golf club, and you can use either side. One result is that Newtonmore has a staggering proportion of ambidextrous men. Fifty per cent of Newtonmore Golf Club are said to be able to play left-handed. The sticks themselves are called clubs though I was unsure later whether this was an allusion to golf or battle.

They can certainly be used for hooking round an opponent's midriff, drawing him towards you and thumping him. This match was not necessarily typical, but it is accepted that shinty is becoming more violent; and halfway through the second half one fight broke out that was not merely off the ball but off the pitch. The referee and a nearby bull mastiff yelped equally helplessly. The game is dangerous enough played properly. The sticks have sharp edges and are inclined to make contact with other sticks and heads with unhappy results for all parties. The sticks, at £13 a time, snap easily – sometimes six a match have to be replaced. The heads are stitched on the National Health.

In spite of everything, no heads were broken at Kiltarlity, only Lovat's pride. Newtonmore scored early, shrugged off an equaliser, and went further and further ahead. One or two of their attacks – the ball curling, high but precise, towards an attacker – were quite beautiful.

Lovat found a harsher reality. After half time they held a committee meeting to discuss a substitution – there are no managers to beckon a man off. 'We've got to take Ally out the defence and put Angy on,' said someone. It was not an impressive demonstration of sporting democracy in action. The argument was still raging when Newtonmore scored their fifth. 'Christ,' said the anti-Ally man, 'that was his fault again.'

Before the end one of the Lovat players, Ian Mackenzie, who travels up every match-day from Middlesbrough, was sent off. Mackenzie, forgive his sins, was born in the village, like everyone else on both sides. That is a point of honour. So is the continuation of the sport.

Shinty is fighting the inroads of soccer and rugby and counter-attacking towards the Lowlands, where in the past it has only been played by Highland exiles. Newtonmore are confident enough to have spent £20,000 resurfacing their pitch. The sport has certainly survived worse crises, nearly dying completely in the last century. Attempted murder by oppressive English, one wondered? Not in the least. It was the kirk. The sterner ministers thought shinty frivolous, like fiddle playing. Even now Newtonmore would not dare play on a Sunday. One can see that Presbyterians of a certain cast of mind might want shinty banned. But frivolous? I think not.

HOW THE CORINTHIANS AND CASUAL FOULING CAN LIVE TOGETHER

November 1981

BARNET 2   CORINTHIAN CASUALS 0

I think this is a damn fine story anyway though I have to admit it would have been a damn sight finer had it been Corinthian Casuals and not Barnet who were going into the FA Cup first round draw today. For Corinthian Casuals just getting this far – the fourth qualifying round – was an extraordinary triumph. In the old days, of course, it would have been nothing. The very name meant imperial sporting splendour and behavioural standards and amateurism.

Yet a few months ago the club had at least one foot and three-quarters in the grave. They had finished bottom of the bottom division of the Isthmian League for the 11th time in 13 years, having won the opening match of the season and none at all after that. The League did not turf them out only because someone else resigned and it seemed rotten to kill such a famous club when it was 99 years old.

Traditionally Corinthians and Casuals (they merged in 1939) recruited players by invitation: good university chaps. And more than 100 of them went on to be either amateur or full internationals. As late as the 1950s they got five-figure gates: they reached the Amateur Cup final in 1956, with eight Cambridge men in the side.

They had to become a little less exclusive. But even so Billy Smith, appointed manager in the summer, was a choice that might have surprised C. B. Fry. Smith used to captain Tooting and Mitcham (whose ground the Casuals share) and sells flowers at Covent Garden. It is tempting to compare him to Eliza Doolittle but in fact he is more like Higgins in reverse: he has transformed the club by teaching it to talk common. Smith's clear-out was almost total. Only one of last season's first team survived. He brought in electricians and telephone engineers – young lads who had knocked around the Isthmian League or Sunday football – and some of the talented Cockney youngsters he worked with in the market.

They were told two things that none of the other Isthmian

151

clubs would tell them. One: they were amateurs. There would be 9p a mile car allowance if there happened to be enough money that week to pay it and nothing else. Two: they were gentlemen. If they got sent off, they would be expelled from the club. Only two Corinthians have ever been sent off and they ceased to be Corinthians at that moment.

Smith's team came to Barnet with five wins and a draw in their last six matches. Their three Cup wins had all been against higher-grade teams but Barnet, from the Alliance Premier, were bound to be their hardest opponents yet. They could have got a draw, they should have got a draw. But Barnet scored after five minutes, withstood some powerful counter-attacks in the second half, and scored the second with a penalty after the Casuals' goalkeeper, Chapman, had *in extremis*, grabbed an opposing leg.

It was the penalty that put the club's traditions under the greatest strain. A little manly fouling is understood to be essential these days but, in the next five minutes, three of their players were booked for arguing.

They have still found themselves a pretty marvellous bunch of lads to see the club through to its centenary. 'It seems to me,' said Bill Wickson, the chairman, 'that the whole of soccer, and probably all sport, is in need of a revival of that strange Corinthian spirit. Now does that sound too awful?'

Sports Diary

February 1982

The second half of the 20th century has finally had its effect on Corinthian Casuals Football Club. In ninety-nine and a half often glorious years only two of their players had ever been sent off. Last week, on a cold night at Egham in the Second Division of the Isthmian League, that total was doubled. Chris Chapman, the goalkeeper, tripped up an opposing forward; Alan Smyth committed two late tackles.

The problem for the club's executive was whether they should adhere to their traditional and inflexible policy by expelling the two from the club. They decided, unanimously, to let them stay. 'This does not mean we have slackened our standards,' said Bill Wickson, the club's chairman. 'If one of our players really did behave in an unsportsmanlike manner, he would be out.'

The Casuals, still strictly amateur, but no longer stuffed with university men, deny that they are inconsistent; they are not so sure about the referees. 'The Casuals were always known for their robust play, shoulder-charging and tackling,' said Alan Jenkins, a member of the executive.

BLIGHT AND SAD TIMES
November 1981
NORTHAMPTON TOWN 1   SHEFFIELD UNITED 2

Finding Sheffield United on top of the Fourth Division is a bit like discovering that one of your old school chums has been put in charge of the prison library. Congratulations, but – er – what are you doing here in the first place? Last night, as so often happens to middle-class prisoners, they were mildly insulted by one of the recidivists. Northampton Town, second from bottom, led them 1-0 until four minutes from the end when United scored two quick, undeserved, but probably preordained goals.

Most of the places United have visited this season are quite new to them, but they have passed this way before – once. It was, believe it or not, a First Division game 16 years ago. They won that too; and I was there, on the terraces or rather the boards they used to sling across the cricket pitch from mid-off to mid-on, with my heavy artillery Northampton rattle. Northampton Town started going to pieces around the time the Borough Council began their scorched earth policy on the town centre. It may be that everything that has happened to the football team since then is some form of planning blight.

The last stages of this match were about the most blighted

there have ever been. Northampton lost 7-1 at Bury on Saturday and have only won one match all season. Yet Northampton did not look the second worst team in the League, nor United a team with seven wins – one over Arsenal – in their last eight matches. Edwards and Hatton, theoretically a considerable pair of strikers, did almost nothing.

There was not a proper shot from anyone until five minutes into the second half when Mahoney of Northampton had a shot punched over the bar by the goalkeeper Waugh (pronounced, this being a long way from Brideshead, Woff). But gradually Phillips, a small, evasive footballer, started to thread his way regularly towards the United goal-line and he scored with a lovely, diving header after 67 minutes.

The Northampton crowd – a large one, considering – did not lapse too far from its long tradition of decorous silence even after this. When Trusson found his way past a disorganised defence to score twice they reverted to the traditional local war cry: 'Rubbish'.

MYSTERIES OF THE EAST AND WEST
December 1981

Although we have passed the stage when every half-wit in Britain fancied himself as a kung-fu expert, the late, great and rather over-the-top actor Bruce Lee has still left a large and confusing legacy of Oriental mayhem.

The Martial Arts Commission, a respectable – almost staid – body affiliated to the Sports Council, is responsible for 11 different sports ranging from karate (by far the most popular, with 100,000 British participants) and taekwando (the Korean variant, which has been wangled into the 1988 Olympics in Seoul) to such arcana as Japanese swordfighting (very popular with intellectuals, apparently), temple boxing and Filipino stickfighting. There is plenty going on inside and outside this empire's frontiers. On Saturday, for example, the

British Men's Team Karate championship was held in Cardiff in accordance with the ideals of the mysterious East and amateur principles. It drew a crowd of 22.

On Sunday, in Edmonton, North London, the Professional Karate Association – unaffiliated – staged an evening of full-contact karate. It drew a crowd of 500 and expressions of extreme distaste whenever it was mentioned in Cardiff. It was held in accordance with the ideals of the mysterious East End and the principle expressed by H.L. Mencken that no one ever went broke underestimating the public's intelligence.

There is in this a fissure infinitely more complicated than in any other sport. People take up karate for one of at least four reasons. Some see it as The Way To Truth and Self-Knowledge, some as a sport, some as a means of self-defence and some as a way to make money. Amateur karate is dominated by the first group, which can make the others very impatient. People go to karate schools hoping to fend off muggers only to find themselves being fed Japanese bafflegab and unable to break bricks – 'Just a silly gimmick,' everyone told me – or heads.

The competition is almost courtly. The fighters execute potentially lethal moves but make no contact, or hardly any. They get points for executing a kick or blow correctly; but if it lands with more than a tap to the body or a very light tap indeed to the head, they are liable to lose a point or even the contest. This is supervised by referees, who often spend more time conferring than refereeing and a doctor so conscientious that you can see the patients wondering when he will give over. It is the reverse of Monday morning surgery.

When the fighters are allowed to continue the blows have to be controlled. It is marvellous discipline. But there is a feeling of punch-up interruptus. The competitors can only really release their emotions by yelling. The spectators are too bored even to do that. Many people are aware of the drawbacks, including David Mitchell, secretary of the Commission, who is pushing a new scoring system to cut out the conferences and encourage the more spectacular moves, and Vic Charles, a 27-year-old Londoner who will probably be the next world champion. Charles is very bright and was

155

rather bolshie even before he became a sociology student, with a habit of short-circuiting karate's stylised training schedules.

Less talented men are easy pickings for full-contact promoters, who offer them money, thrills, glamour and money. The Professional Karate Association is American, organised in Europe by a London-based Greek, George Sfetas, who in 15 months has managed to overshadow some of the dodgier operators. He uses a lot of American hype and boasts big-name backers, like Jack Nicholson and George Peppard. (We know Peppard is keen because we asked him. 'I enjoy watching it,' he said. 'It's like ferocious ballet.') David Mitchell, who is in charge of amateur full-contact, does not even approve of that. 'I think it's brutal,' he said.

I was sufficiently forewarned to wear old clothes to Edmonton in case of bloodstains. The crowd seemed to have the same idea. They looked macho but vacant; more like The Den than Zen. The fighters mostly need the money. But until they have had six fights, they don't get any. Many of them never reach six, especially those trained in non-combat karate who sometimes have trouble remembering that this time the blows are going to land. It can be a painful lesson. The survivors can earn maybe a couple of hundred a fight.

The trappings bear no relation to conventional karate. There are no mats, bowing or judo regalia. There are seconds, a ring and gloves. The fighters must land eight kicks above the waist per two-minute round; often they treat them as a chore then get on with the business of punching hell out of each other. Then it just becomes crude boxing. On the whole, there did not seem to be any more blood or danger than on some boxing bills. Rather less, according to the ring-side doctor, because more blows were aimed to the body than the head. The audience thought differently. They worked themselves into a state of such hysteria that it appeared safer inside the ring. As usual, the women were the more bloodthirsty.

Sfetas was one of the chief screamers. He is not a bad bloke. But he 'looks after' certain of the fighters while at the same time running the whole competition. He answers that he also supervises the lighting and puts on the cassettes and other people are lazy and somebody has to do the work or this sport will never get off the ground. If Sfetas gets rich, he will have earned his money. He had better hope, though, that no one distracts his followers by coming up with something really vicious: Thai kick boxing, for instance, in which almost anything does go; Lions v Christians; or possibly re-enactments of Pearl Harbor. At least that would be authentically Japanese.

SCENES FROM BRUEGEL ENLIVEN THE FENS
December 1981

There are two ways of regarding this weather. There is the school of Bruegel the Elder and Queen's Park Rangers, which holds that you ought to be out there in the cold enjoying yourself. Personally, I lean towards the school of British Rail, which holds that it is better to stay indoors, assume the foetal position and hope it blows over.

The weekend, however, provided some evidence for the opposition. The same isotherms that savaged the rest of sport permitted the staging of the Duddleston Cup, the most important trophy in Fenland skating. It not only provided some of the day's best sport, but maintained a rich and happy local tradition.

Fenland is a cold part of Britain, bedevilled by what they call the lazy wind (too lazy to go round you, so it goes through you). Before they were drained, there were loads of fens to skate on. Even now, the locals seem to take naturally to the sport. They even have their own makeshift Wembley. At the start of December the water board opens the sluices on the River Glen and floods a meadow at Baston, north of Peterborough. Then everyone waits. Last winter, there was almost no skating at all. This winter, a couple of cold nights were enough. The skates and cups came out of warm storage and everyone headed for Baston.

There are enough traditional competitions to last a small Ice Age. Some of them have not been contested since the 1940s. But they like to run the Duddleston if they can. It is open to speed skaters from all over Britain, and they got 14 of them, including John French and John Tipper, who were in the last Olympics, and one local lad who agreed to make up the numbers. Many of the best skaters were elsewhere, concentrating on an indoor event, which involves constant tight turning round a small rink. But Fen skating is much more like the Olympic skill. The course is 440 yards round. A mile is the standard distance with the skaters running two at a time in lanes instead of jostling for position.

Some things are not quite Olympic. The entries are taken by Fen farmers, in cloth caps and gumboots, sitting on straw bales. The course is marked out by wood blocks and old oil drums. Even the ice has its imperfections, where the wind rippled the water as it froze. The best of the skaters do the mile in just over two and a half minutes. Sebastian Coe, running alongside would be lapped even if he stayed upright. Eric Heiden, the Olympic champion, might do nearer two minutes if he could cope with the chancy surface.

The heats are time trials rather than races, which takes some of the fun away. But French and Tipper were paired together in the final, and they produced a genuinely thrilling race. They made an odd sight, standing in their kinky skintight gear like out-of-work divers, crouching like crones (to minimise the wind resistance) as they race. French took the lead round the final bend and won by four-fifths of a second to general approval. He is a Fen boy, who learned to skate in the bad – or good – winter of 1963 and, though he has spent a lot of time training abroad, he loves the tradition and is glad to be home.

That race did distract the crowd. Most of them, including some quite elderly parties, had been too busy skating or tobogganing themselves to watch the others. From a distance, the whole scene was much as Bruegel would have painted it, with thin sunlight picking out the few reeds and clods of frozen earth that had escaped the enveloping whiteness.

French had to be given the wrong cup because the

Duddleston had not been contested for three years, and no one could immediately lay their hands on it. They will work through as many other cups as they can find until the thaw sets in. I was sufficiently enchanted by it all to put aside my own feelings and tell the organiser, Eric Fisher, that I hoped it kept cold for him. 'I don't know about that,' he said. 'I'm a farmer. I've got a lot of taters getting frozen.'

LESSONS TO LEARN FROM PANTHERS' PROWL
February 1982

This is primarily a piece about ice hockey but it needs to be put in context with a piece of news which I promise you is relevant and you may have missed. Last week the Football League managers and secretaries voted by 113 votes to 44 in favour of summer soccer. Consider two further facts: Notts County, newly promoted in the First Division, who in less successful days packed 47,000 into Meadow Lane, have had one crowd this season as low as 6,292 and an average that is not much higher. A mile up the road at the ice rink Nottingham Panthers are filling every seat every week.

Admittedly the rink only holds 2,800. But the tickets go on sale at 2 p.m. on Mondays and the queue starts forming by 9.45. It is said – though the rink manager, Malcolm Balchin, thinks this is a bit of an exaggeration – that if you are not there by 10.30 you cannot be sure of a seat. Often all the tickets go in 15 minutes. It is not unreasonable to suppose that if, by some technological miracle, Meadow Lane could be satisfactorily iced over, the Panthers would attract rather more than 6,292. It is perhaps time to rethink our ideas about major and minor sport.

The Panthers only re-formed last season, a spin-off from the team in Sheffield. In the days when Britain had a professional circuit, the Panthers were among the mainstays – they won the National League three times in the 1950s. But the circuit collapsed. The management of the Nottingham rink refused to countenance any more hockey until Balchin took over two years ago and restarted both the game and the special hockey clock which had stood above the rink, stopped and mouldering, for 20 years.

This season the Panthers are challenging Streatham Redskins as the country's leading side. But they were getting full houses with a more ordinary side last year. Gary Keward, their manager – a Nottingham lad who spent 19 years in Canada – thinks it is a mixture of local tradition and publicity. The papers and radio stations ring him every day as if he were Brian Clough. The stadium was even full last Saturday for the match with Cambridge University in the English League (South), just about the weakest team in the least important competition. One-sided ice hockey is very non-exciting and the Panthers were able to experiment and still win 19-1.

The atmosphere was nostalgic, even for those who could not remember the old hockey days. The rink dates back to before the war; it is probably the last major stadium in Britain where you can buy loose aniseed balls. They play the National Anthem on the organ before the match. The spectators blow horns when the Panthers score and applaud when the opposition does. Had there been a few rattles it might have been a 1950s soccer crowd. For me, they destroyed the theory that violence on the field is connected with violence off it. Even this uncompetitive match had players regularly dispatched to the sidelines for 'unnecessary roughing'. (And what, pray, is necessary roughing?) Yet the crowd might have been watching a chamber orchestra.

Ice hockey has other things to teach soccer. After years of somnambulism, it is returning to prominence on a far more sensible financial basis than before. The players are amateurs; at Nottingham, only the rink is getting rich. None of this means that ice hockey is about to displace soccer nationally. Skating is a hard enough skill for the average British lad to acquire without having to learn how to play hockey and fight simultaneously. Anyway, the rinks do not exist. Other clubs do not get Nottingham's attendances and

160

the best guess is that Brighton is the only town where the phenomenon could be repeated – and there is no suitable rink there.

But soccer ought to take notice. If a successful team in Nottingham struggles to compete against ice hockey and the handful of other diversions of winter, what earthly chance would it have against cricket, tennis, golf, walking in the park, digging the garden, dozing in the sun and the thousand mixed blessings of summer. A few years ago, when summer soccer was mentioned, people would mutter 'Oh, be a shame, ruin cricket.' You would have to be a cosmic twit – or live in the cocooned world of a football manager – to believe that now. Nottingham ice hockey is merely a warning like the cock crowing at sundown before an earthquake. Beneath our feet, the entire fabric of British sport is starting to tremble and shift.

CHUKKAS OUT OF BEACHCOMBER
May 1982

In case the rush of other news prevented the BBC doing its traditional Bank Holiday duty last night, you should be informed at once that the Prince of Wales' team, the Diables Bleus, won their opening match in the Queen's Cup polo competition 8-6 against a team called the BBs at Windsor yesterday. The Queen's Cup is traditionally the first major competition of the season and was observed yesterday with plenty of the traditional *élan* and Bollinger. But this season is not normal. The Argentines are missing.[1]

Usually about a dozen of their players come over for the summer. Polo people insist that their absence makes no difference. On further questioning this is revised to not very much difference. Evidently a number of women were banking on their arrival. On the field, certainly, the Argentines are the world's best. The rich ones have plenty of horses and plenty of open spaces to ride them as well as plenty of the mad buggers' daring that enables men of their class and nation to fly suicide missions in Mirages. Such daring is crucial in polo.

Prince Charles is genuinely good. Only seven other Britons have better handicaps and they must have more time to practise. It takes horsemanship, ball-sense and guts, though that is all useless without a suitable mount. The horses, mostly runtish thoroughbreds, need speed and guts too. They can be hit by a hard ball, a mallet or another horse at 30 mph. They can last only one chukka at a time, which is why players must have a string of them and why the sport is so expensive.

I found much the same stamina problem as the horses. The pitch was huge, the ball was small and unless you were Royalty or the *Daily Mail*, who for some reason had their own stand, the seats were rock hard. It should really have been not the *Mail*, but the *Express*: most of the people seemed to have stepped straight out of dear old Beachcomber. The BBs included Tony Devcich, Major Reddy Watt and Somerville Livingstone-Learmonth. And there are only four in a team.

I looked around for the Harbour Master of Grustiwowo Bay and indeed he might have been sitting quietly in the members' stand. Plenty of equally unreal characters stepped onto the field at half time (after three chukkas) which is sounded as in Rugby League by a hooter. However, you cannot slope off for a Bovril and a jimmy. You are expected to go on and tread down the divots. This is the nearest polo ever gets to being a mass participation sport.

[1] Note the date: the Falklands war was on.

SULKY NIGHT AT THE HIPPODROME
July 1982

Clem Dodd marked his 67th birthday by giving a three-year-old colt called White Star a couple of sharp reminders and driving it home to victory. To add to the statistics it might have been Clem's 5,000th winner. He thought that sounded about right. But his first winner came when he was 13, and in this branch of horseracing no one has ever kept count properly. We were walking in the paddock after Clem had given White Star his rub. There were no stables or grass there but a lot of small boulders. Ascot it was not. It was – and this may surprise people who have lived there all their lives – Droylsden Races.

There are a number of differences between Droylsden, where Manchester has a last fling at being ugly before giving way to the Pennines, and the big Flat tracks. The most fundamental is that Droylsden stages harness races: trotting and pacing contests between horses pulling chariots known as sulkies. It has staged them since 1928 when the races were mainly between butchers' nags. Since then harness racing has grown into a huge sport and industry – in America, Australasia, and much of Europe. In Canada, trotting is bigger than what they call, with some contempt, galloping. In Britain, the trots are big only in the Labour Party. At Droylsden, the butchers' nags would now be outpaced. But they would still feel at home.

There are two mysteries about British harness racing. One – why it has failed so completely to take off. Two – given that it has failed, how it survives at all. The economics are horrendous. It costs almost as much to keep a harness horse (they are known as standardbreds) in training as it does a thoroughbred. They eat the same. Yet the prize money is around the level of the dog tracks: £70 for the top race at Droylsden; £2,000 for the top race of the year, the Musselburgh Pace in Scotland.

The only ways to get rich are by breeding an outstanding horse and selling it overseas, which is a slim chance, or by keeping one step ahead of the bookmakers, which seemed an even slimmer chance at Droylsden as they were offering the meanest prices seen since Honest Eb Scrooge (No Credit: No Each Way) hung up his satchel. Not many people were there to bet with them anyway, though they have always raced on summer Mondays at Droylsden – it used to be butchers' early closing. A small crowd flitted between the stands and the unpretentious bar. Far more people were playing squash, oblivious, in the young-executive-type club at the back.

The horses have their gait bred and trained into them: a lateral, rolling movement for pacers; a diagonal, slightly slower, more mincing movement for trotters. Just in case, the pacers wear hobbles round their legs to make sure they can't gallop – not cruel though rather inconvenient. What with the reins and the harness and all the other gubbins, the effect is to make the horses look like Clapham Junction.

Overall, I was reminded of the Olympic walking races in which gallant, slightly cracked Brits used to do rather well. You are forbidden to do the obvious thing, which is to go flat out, but you can work up a pretty fair lick none the less. At 30 mph round a small track it was more exciting than squinting at horses emerging from the distance at Newmarket, the more so when Len Dilloway, who has trained winners at Flat, harness, and pony racing, kindly tipped me a 4-1 winner.

At that speed there is some danger. The accidents can be spectacular: a sprawl of cartwheels, horseflesh, and human. Poor Clem Dodd will never move his right wrist again. But this sport is in his blood – his uncle built the track – and the younger men still respect his horsemanship.

Several people said it was a shame I came to Droylsden, litter-strewn and down-at-heel, instead of one of the nicer meetings like York or Kendal or up to Scotland, where the sport thrives better. Someone else said the whole game has been spoiled by the 'gypsy and scrap metal fraternity' if I got his drift. If that was a roundabout reference to trickery, I can only say that I did not spot any. The sport now has a proper rule book, Stud Book and Racing Calendar – all the trappings of the Jockey Club except that the stewards' room at Droylsden had loads of brown ale bottles, which suggests they keep comparatively sober.

Anyway, there is not too much room for hocus-pocus when the bookmakers have a 5-4 on shot, an even money, and three 4-1 shots in the same race. 'If there's betting, you can be sure there's something going on,' said Len Dilloway. 'This is no worse than Flat racing. It doesn't matter whether you race mice or snails, there's always something.'

THE TANGLED ROOTS OF COUSIN JOHN
September 1983

It is roots season in Dublin just now; with the punt roughly at par with the Peruvian cocoa bean, let alone the dollar, the hotels are fuller than ever with rich Americans trying to find their ancestry. Politicians come to Ireland for this even if their name is Goldblum.

Fifty slow miles up the road to County Cavan, it is sheep dipping time at Ballyjamesduff (winner of Ireland's tidy town competition 1966-67). The significance of this is the first visit to Ireland of the world's most famous Irish-American and certainly the most famous son, or at any rate grandson of Ballyjamesduff. John McEnroe has arrived.

Regrettably, he will not be coming to Ballyjamesduff on this trip. He is in Dublin on business; and he is taking it seriously even if it is not, by his normal standard, especially serious business. The United States are playing the Irish in the Davis Cup. As a result of Italy beating Ireland and Argentina beating the US, this is a relegation contest. It is of course unthinkable that the Americans could lose. McEnroe, who loses money but gains merit marks by agreeing to play in this competition, would be expected to win his three matches if he were bolted to the floor of the New York Yacht Club. But this is not a week when the United States are disposed to take anything in sport for granted.[1]

Should Ireland win, McEnroe could also switch sides. When the teams lined up he was, with his tousled hair and snub nose, the only player who looked Irish. This was not an illusion. The two official Irishmen are Sean Sorensen, McEnroe's singles opponent tonight, and Matt Doyle, who plays Elliott Teltscher tonight and McEnroe on Sunday. Sorensen was brought up in Cork but was born in Maine, lives in West Germany and has Norwegian ancestors. Doyle's qualification is a great-grandparent who emigrated from Kerry to California and a sufficiently whimsical manner to take Sorensen's suggestion that he could play for Ireland seriously.

McEnroe is one generation closer than Doyle. But he has

yet to get the hang of Irishness. When someone mentioned his grandparents living in Cavan, he gave a look which implied, 'Whaddya mean, they lived in a cavern?' There is also the matter of temperament. One can sympathise with him. Airports, hotel suites and tennis courts look much the same in Dublin as they do anywhere else; and if anything, the paparazzi are even more persistent and the local sponsors' speeches even more boring. This one was delivered by a Mr Nakamura.

Though McEnroe has yet to find his roots, some purported roots are trying very hard to find him. The tie, being staged in a hall more regularly used for showjumping, is a sellout of sellouts; officials reckon that if any of the 6,000 tickets reached the black market, they would fetch £200. So far, at least 3,000 people have rung up and announced that they are McEnroes from Cavan and would like tickets.

The expert on the subject is supposed to be McEnroe's lawyer father. He has unearthed plenty of relatives on his mother's side from Westmeath and invited them to a little do at the hotel last night, with the parade led by John's 85-year-old great-aunt Molly. But he has not yet been to Ballyjamesduff, where there are still plenty of McEnroes in the phone book as well as in the graveyard. None of them seems to be clamouring to watch the tennis.

Three generations ago McEnroes farmed land for miles around. But hard times got even harder and John's grandfather and all his brothers left for America. The family farm was knocked down. The closest relative now appears to be John's third cousin, Cornelius, and his mother, Phyllis, who is not much interested in tennis or her unruly kinsman. 'Sure, but he's got a terrible temper. I'd put him over my knee and give him a good clattering.'

Ballyjamesduff is not really a John McEnroe sort of town. Yesterday, everyone was walking around saying 'nice day,' 'grand,' when it palpably was not. It is a quiet town in the hills, where Colm's bar doubles as the funeral parlour, and on a damp autumn Thursday an unsentimental youth might mistake it for the pits of the world.

McEnroe is anxious to see a bit of Ireland but as soon as this

tie finishes, he has to play exhibitions in Canada. His younger
brothers have already been here: Patrick played in several
Irish junior tournaments; Mark did a year studying politics at
Trinity College. It can take a year to explore the intricacies of
Erin: The Book of Kells, the Kings of Tara and the telephone
system. John will never be able to do that. He is doomed to
fame and recognition, presumably for life. 'We don't
complain about that,' said his father, 'it comes with the
territory.' But as McEnroe sat, more successfully than some of
us, trying to remember his manners during Mr Nakamura's
interminable speech, one could feel no envy for all his money,
glory and fame. He looked young, lonely and vulnerable. If
they ever do meet, cousin Phyllis will probably take the same
view.

[1] The US had just lost the America's Cup.

A CASE OF PLUCK IT AND SEE
April 1986

Fort de France, Martinique: There are places in the Caribbean
where they are not laughing at England and its cricketers. An
hour's flight from Barbados and sandwiched between two
more cricket-bonkers islands, St Lucia and Dominica, is
Martinique. And if anyone here has been rattling on about
Gower and Botham, then my O-level French (somewhat
rusted) failed to catch it.

Martinique not only feels like France warmed up; it is
France. When Britain's colonies started to make their own
way in the world, the French West Indies nuzzled closer to La
Grande Patrie and became incorporated. This is the EEC and
any Martiniquais, unlike a Barbadian or a Jamaican, can settle
in London. Since the island is awash with Paris government
cash and full mainland social security rates and is very
beautiful as well, Heathrow is unlikely to be overwhelmed by
the rush.

Among the *charcuteries* and *épiceries* of town, it is hard to imagine this is not Marseilles or somewhere. But sport here is not just boules and yellow jerseys. I discovered the truth about Martinique by using the cunning resourceful methods of the true investigative reporter. I looked in the guide book. And there it was – national sport: cock-fighting; combats most days between January and July, ask the tourist office. So I did.

Now all this seemed very strange, as though *England on 25 Dollars A Day* advised readers to go down to Stamford Bridge for the headkicking. Britain made cock-fighting illegal in 1849. But the book was right. And on what should have been the final day of the Bridgetown West Indies v England bear-bait I found myself at the Pitt Marceni, 10 miles from the capital Fort de France, in a barn among the cornfields.

The Marceni is not the most imposing arena in the sport. Cock-fighting was huge business in pre-Castro Cuba, still is in Haiti, while Puerto Rico is said to have a super-stadium with air-conditioning, Astroturf and restaurant-cum-cocktail lounge. This, though, was how I always imagined a cockpit, the kind of thing Henry VIII and Charles II must have known. About 100 people sat snugly under the tin roof in galleries, while down below two cocks tried to kill each other.

The entertainment, if that is the word, is shortlived compared to the preliminaries. For up to half an hour before each main contest, the bets are struck while the handlers prepare their charges, the final stage of a training process almost as old as time. Fighting cocks are kept like racehorses and often fed on filet mignon. They are plucked close to give the other bird as little leverage as possible; underneath the wing they look oven-ready. Then, at Marceni, while the 200 franc notes flew, the last rites were applied. The birds were washed with ether to detect any hint of grease on the remaining plumage, which would be a cheat; artificial spurs were added for extra spiking power and the birds were dangled to keep them quiet.

The smell of the ether rose and mingled with the stale sweat and Gauloises. Everyone, bird and man, wore a knowing, expectant look. Suddenly, the seconds were out of the ring, the doors slammed and a bell rang. Rouge v. noir et blanc. For a moment the cocks appeared as though they would ignore each other, do the sensible thing and wander off, pecking.

But then their hackles rose. First it was an eyeball confrontation with a flutter of wings. Then a game of leapfrog. Finally rouge grabbed hold with its beak and began to tear at its opponent's neck with the spurs. Cock-fighting is essentially a gouging contest. Sometimes you could hear an effective set of combination-gouges going in. But usually it was drowned, by the crowd screaming '*Allez, allez*' and placing late bets. One moment, the birds were at each other on the dusty ground. Then they shot skywards simultaneously and dug in again. The techniques of Saturday afternoon wrestling vied with the instincts of murder. The battle lasted almost 10 minutes and ended with what looked like a pinfall. Noir et blanc won, but both birds were taken away as red, raw messes.

The second contest was quicker and the winner stood on top of the loser, as though he were the referee administering the count. After the third, both birds, victor and vanquished, so sleek at the start, looked dead. It would not, apparently, be unusual if they were. Another dozen contests were scheduled but already the pit was spattered with feathers and blood. By the end it would look like a charnel house. It was time to go.

The intricacies were explained to me later by Raul Depaz, a retired rum baron, president of the AFM, the governing body, and the Vincent O'Brien of Martiniquais cock-fighting. He is a man of great charm and cultivation, not at all like the furtive figures with long sideburns who occasionally get arrested after closing time deep in some Home Counties woods. I expressed surprise. 'In England,' said Mr Depaz, 'I think people higher than me fight cocks.'

Mr Depaz gets some criticism from anti-cruelty organisations in France; rather less in Martinique itself where up to 40,000 cocks fight every year and the sport constitutes a substantial industry. He showed me his battery cages where the young chicks are already starting to scratch each other: 'The instinct is bred into them.' He disapproves of the version on Guadelupe where the artificial spurs are of steel rather than the sharpened offcuts of dead birds. Fights there rarely last more than 30 seconds and the penalty of defeat is invariably death.

Gamecocks have been bred to destroy each other for thousands of years. They know no other way. The ancient Persians were at it, and the Greeks and the Romans. In Regency England it was a school sport. There are still primeval undertones: one of Mr Depaz's breeding techniques involves incest, champion father with daughter, and he said something about the importance of the phases of the moon.

I decided to skip Martinique's other traditional offering: mongoose v serpent. At dinner, I refrained from ordering the *coq au vin*.

MANILA LEADS THE BRAVE A MERRY DANCE
November 1986

Santa Anita, California: The Union Jack was gloomily lowered in a sunlit corner of the globe yet again at the weekend when Dancing Brave, widely, fondly and perhaps still accurately believed to be one of the greatest racehorses ever trained in Britain, ended his career in unequivocal defeat. He came only fourth in the $2 million Breeders' Cup turf race, beaten almost seven lengths by Manila, who is also a son of Lyphard and owned by a Kentucky bloodstock dealer called Mike Shannon, who sold Dancing Brave as a yearling and is now cheerfully convinced he made the right decision.

The British contingent began to sense disaster as soon as Pat Eddery rounded the near hairpin bend at the end of the back straight. There was no burst of acceleration as in all his other races, even his defeat in the Derby – no hint of imperiousness. The Brave could not even get close to the local mare Estrapade, who came third, while the real battle was fought between Manila and Theatrical, second in the Irish Derby last year, when trained by Dermot Weld, but not a horse, on any previous reckoning, in Dancing Brave's division. Manila got up to win by a neck.

Dancing Brave still won about £100,000 – seven per cent of the purse – for coming fourth, so his owner, Khalid Abdulla, will survive. After winning eight races out of 10, including the 2,000 Guineas, the King George and the Arc, the colt's winnings have just squeezed over the £1 million mark.

After the race came one of those jockey-trainer conversations between Eddery and Guy Harwood which consist mostly of gesticulations and shrugs. The significant sign language comprised Eddery flicking one hand fast against the other to indicate that the horse would not respond to his steering round the turn. Harwood was philosophical and consoling; it may be imagination, but I thought the saddest looking figure in the tableau was the horse. Dancing Brave, however, was not available for quotes.

Harwood thought the problems of the track and his long, hard season, had made the difference. 'I was worried earlier in the week that he had lost his zip.' Eddery added with some bitterness: 'These other horses couldn't beat him with a hammer in Europe.'

But it was no day to extol European racing – the Brits were the ones who got hammered in every race they entered – and along came Shannon, a million bucks to the good, chewing gum and looking and sounding rather like Rod Steiger playing a Southern cop and bullying Sidney Poitier. 'I kept the best one. Horse of the Year. Horse of the Century? I wasn't that impressed by the Arc. Mine might just be the best horse we've seen in the United States in years.'

Shannon bought Manila from Edward Cojuangco, a Filipino beer baron and crony of ex-President Marcos, who sold all his horses when the regime collapsed. 'He's named after the greatest city I have ever been to in the world.' Shannon added, with as straight a face as his gum allowed. 'I hope Mr Marcos gets to go back there some time.'

Dancing Brave now goes to stud near Newmarket and the defeat is especially bad news for the breeders who chipped into the £14 million stud syndicate, but in the long run it may also be bad news for the people anxious to turn this event into a sort of transglobal equine Superbowl. Like Nijinsky, Shergar and Troy, Dancing Brave has tried nobly and just

171

failed to turn a three-year-old season that starts in the spring into a triumphal procession all autumn. Next year this event will be held three weeks later (at the nearby Hollywood Park track) and even if 1987 throws up a British horse of Dancing Brave's quality, the connections are likely to think twice and three times before risking the trip.

But it was one heck of a day's racing. Sixty-nine thousand people turned up; $15 million, a North American record, was bet on the monopolist Tote (a fair chunk of that, one suspects, invested by British bookmakers anxious to keep Dancing Brave's price down – he started at 2-1 on); even the smog co-operated and lifted to provide a golden afternoon and a glorious view of the mountains. The customary race crowd was augmented by some very high class San Fernando Valley princesses and a sprinkling of British racing types in chalk-stripes and titfers. For most of them it was an expensive exercise.

In the $3 million classic on the dirt track, overshadowed even for most Americans by Dancing Brave's race, but still the richest event in the sport, Pat Eddery was out with the washing on Clive Brittain's Bold Arrangement behind the locally-trained Skywalker. The one Euro coup of the day was landed by the French trainer Robert Collet, whose carefully-laid scheme to switch Last Tycoon from sprinting was rewarded with a 35-1 win in the Turf Mile. Michael Stoute's entry, Sonic Lady, came seventh with no excuses. In the sprint Double Schwartz, fancied by his stable, and Green Desert filled the last two places. All very sad. Damn it, even our cricket teams usually manage to finish as runners-up.

HORSEPLAY AT HANGING ROCK
January 1987

Hanging Rock, Victoria: The film *Picnic at Hanging Rock*, you may recall, was a story about the disappearance of two turn-of-the-century Australian schoolgirls; the whole thing being a mixture of history, mystery, fable, long summer dresses, soft-focus photography and general upmarket directors' hokum.

The real picnic at Hanging Rock takes place twice a year and involves the more down-to-earth mystery of why humankind wastes so much time, energy, and money on such an unreliable beast as the racehorse. But somehow the experience of losing money was much less painful than usual; Hanging Rock is one of the most unexpected, friendliest and loveliest racetracks on earth.

Picnic racing anywhere is one of the great Aussie institutions. There are little meetings on summer days all over Australia in places with names like Tatura, Towong, and Yanko Creek. There is the Great Western meeting held where they make the local champagne; the racegoers usually go on winery tours first and afterwards behave accordingly. And there is a place called Bong-Bong, where the meeting has passed into folklore as a byword for yobbery.

Hanging Rock, though, is famously good-tempered. Perhaps people are inspired by the setting: the volcanic pinnacles of the rock towering above them, the gum trees and hills of Victoria stretching ahead of them, and the sheer brooding resonance of the place, which is sacred to the Wurrunjerrie (or River Gum Grub) tribe as well as to the Australian film industry. More likely, everyone behaves because the big meeting is held on New Year's Day, and they are all much too subdued after the night before to get too raucously drunk.

Technically, Hanging Rock is not really a picnic meeting because the jockeys are pros (if not exactly the local Edderys and Carsons) and the whole thing is run by the official stewards. But everyone thinks of it as picnic racing – a day out in the country, an hour's drive from Melbourne. And if it were a normal meeting it would have been killed off years ago by bureaucratic officials as uneconomic, outdated and even dangerous – it's a very tight track and nasty and greasy if it rains. The meeting has been kept going by its enormous popularity and its sense of tradition. This year saw the 101st running of the Hanging Rock Cup.

The nearest English equivalent is a point-to-point meeting, which is the epitome, if not the epicentre, of our forelock-tugging class system: rich farmer in his Porsche, the poor man in his scruff. At Hanging Rock, the next Toyota could contain the governor of Victoria and I don't suppose anyone would be the wiser unless they had seen him on television.

Just about everyone else was there this year on the sort of summer's day that might have been ordained for the inaugural running of the Garden of Eden Derby: 70 degrees, not a cloud in sight, and just a whiff of breeze.

The horses were slightly less than perfect. Melbourne trainers use the Rock as a last resort for their less responsive pupils. 'If they can't win here,' one explained, 'there's not much they'll be able to do in this area. You have to sell them to Queensland or West Australia, where the standard's lower. After that, it's Darwin or Alice Springs. After that, it's the can of Pal.' Even the horses must realise they are not at Royal Ascot. They are housed in what look like bicycle sheds and are paraded on the track while kids play cricket a few yards away, hurriedly drawing the stumps when the horses turn to go down to the start. One or two of the entrants in the lesser handicaps look as though they could do with a picnic themselves, and one dull specimen so resolutely refused to move that it had to be led while the poor jockey jogged behind.

You can't even see the races very well. There is no stand, grand or otherwise, and for much of the race the horses are out of sight behind the gum trees. It is hard to see even from the top of the Rock, and I couldn't understand a word the commentator said. The best vantage point is the koala's-eye-view up in the trees themselves. But the koalas have this place more or less to themselves, except for a few passing humans and bush wallabies on the 363 non-racing days of the year; they are notoriously ratty about the invasion of privacy and go all sulky, climbing higher in the trees to escape and doze or, occasionally, having a good, vengeful spit.

Everyone else enjoys themselves thoroughly because it really is such a grand day out. They park themselves in their deckchairs so you can hardly reach the bookies. And they come back year after year. George Olden, now 76, has seen every Hanging Rock Cup, except when his country called him, since 1915. He remembers when the fairground, which now has inflated castles and rides on fire engines, used to have boxing booths and Hawaiian hula girls with suspiciously Aussie accents and skin tones.

He also recalls the great Sydney Cup scam of the 1920s. The stewards used to ride in their buggy to the nearby pub, which had the only telephone in the area, to get the result of what everyone outside Hanging Rock thought was the day's big race. With the help of a co-operative telephone operator, who stalled the stewards, and the first fast car in the district, some local wide boys managed to get back to the course with late money for a very nice 200-1 winner.

The course now has computerised access to the state-wide tote system and video-recorders to stop any hanky-panky. But it's still wonderfully chummy: I was introduced to everyone; they all had time for me, told me racing tales and (in several cases) swore blind that their great-aunt had known someone who insisted that, yes, two schoolgirls really had disappeared there and never been seen again. I asked my mate George about this. 'It's a load of baloney,' he said. 'My grandmother remembered the Kelly gang coming through here. I think she'd have mentioned it.'

MIDSUMMER RITES AND RAIN
June 1988

The traditional figures in white returned to the ancient shrine yesterday to celebrate the solstice at the annual midsummer festival. As at similar mystical gatherings, adherents hark back to heroes from a semi-mythical period of British glory. At Stonehenge it is Merlin; at Wimbledon it is Fred Perry.

In accordance with the rite, the ceremony began at the

moment the clock in the hallowed ring – known as Centre Court – reached two. Then came the incantation 'Quiet please, first set, ready, play.' At that moment a beardless youth is offered as sacrifice to the deity. On this occasion it meant that Todd Woodbridge, an Australian who looked at least 12 years old, was obliged to play tennis against Pat Cash, which he did briefly.

In the adjoining circle, the victim was British, which is more in accordance with the ancient folk ways. David Felgate, the 362nd best player in the world, was obliged to play Ivan Lendl, the best, to similar effect. After the match Felgate had to endure the worst part of the ordeal: attending the interview room. There, against a backdrop incongruously borrowed from a railway station photo booth, he was decent and gracious. This is also part of the rite, though it has been largely forgotten in recent years.

But Britain is not finished yet. It will be represented in the second round, which is more than can be said for, say, Mali. Their only player, Yaya Doubia, has gone in straight sets. They have never beaten us at either soccer or cricket and I bet their hooligans are useless too.

And, say what you like about British tennis, we do put on a splendid tournament. In places like Virginia Water, they think it's all about Virginia Wade and Virginia creeper. Actually, it's more about Virginia Slims and everyone else in the corporate sponsorship business. But the rustic illusions are maintained with great skill. If you wander among the yew hedges and the hydrangeas, carefully keeping the perimeter razor wire out of the corner of your eye, it remains possible to imagine this is the very picture of Merrie Olde England, provided your picture of Merrie Olde England includes champagne at £24.50 a bottle and strawberries at five bob each.

In general, the first day of Wimbledon was based on variations of the time-honoured themes. Sixteen ticket touts were arrested for obstruction, including one with a cordless phone who was believed to be the first designer tout. He indignantly protested that he was a 'ticket broker'.

There was a hint of erotica: the photographers became

very agitated after hearing that the American Barbara Potter had hurriedly changed her top on an outside court without informing them first. And at six o'clock, as no doubt happened in the times of both Fred Perry and Merlin, it began to drizzle.

A TINY TURK WHO MADE LIGHT OF THE WORLD
September 1988

Seoul: Perhaps the most remarkable physical specimen of them all at these Olympics duly collected his gold medal last night. There was never much doubt that he would win once he was here, least of all in his own mind. In advance, however, there were a number of questions – like which name he would use, which country he would represent and whether he would be allowed to compete at all.

The man's name now is Naim Suleymanoglu, and he won the weight-lifting in the 60 kg category – that's featherweight – by lifting more than three times his own bodyweight above his head to give Turkey its first gold medal since 1968. Two years ago he was Naum Shalamonov of Bulgaria, having been forced to change his name as part of the Bulgarians' policy of forcing conformity on their Muslim Turkish minority.

Two years ago he quietly slipped away while competing in Australia, went to Turkey, changed his name back to Suleymanoglu and became an important symbolic figure in matters of Balkan ethnicity. Politically, we are back in areas that have not worried British newspaper readers since 1918; one half-feels that it is necessary to analyse the relevance to relations between Serbia and Austria-Hungary.

In weightlifting terms, however, Suleymanoglu has gone so far into the future that no one can possibly keep up. He is only four foot ten tall and he weighs nine stone six. To win the gold, he broke either an Olympic or his own world record with each of his six lifts. In the snatch – the part where they have to lift the weight with one clean movement – his last effort was 152.5 kg or 24 stone. No other man has ever snatched two and a half times his own weight. In the clean and jerk – when competitors are allowed to take an understandable breather with the load at shoulder level – he finished at 190 kg, or 30 stone. That is two kilograms more than his old world record, and equivalent to holding up Cyril Smith plus a healthy five-year-old. Thirty years ago even the heavyweights could not do that; the man is amazing.

Under Olympic eligibility rules, the Bulgarians could have kept Suleymanoglu out of Seoul, as he has not been in Turkey long enough. That would have ensured them their third weight-lifting gold out of three awarded so far – their own man Stefan Topourov was the only person to come within a mile of the winner. They were surprisingly decent about it, apparently for three reasons. First, Bulgaria, more than any other East European state, take their cue from Moscow, and beastliness is suddenly out of fashion there. Secondly, Sofia was a candidate for the 1994 Winter Olympics and needed to impress the IOC. Thirdly, the Bulgarians are rumoured to have received a pay-off of around £750,000 – the first transfer fee, as someone put it, in the history of weight-lifting.

The Bulgarians do take this sport rather seriously. It is said that one of their techniques is to put their lifters on a drip-feed to build them up – after the weigh-in. Bulgaria have several more weight-lifting stars to come this week. But they will never forget the one that got away.

Topourov knew he was licked. Like all the weight-lifters he is exceptional himself. In this division there is nothing to any of them except sinew, thighs and buttocks. (Heaven knows what some of them take, but I don't think it's Dextrosol.) Suleymanolgu is an astonishing sight: facially he is rather impish, sort of boyishly handsome. He has the torso of a circus midget – but his thighs are like traffic bollards. He is also a considerable showman. He walks out to perform his routine with measured tread and almost grins as he lifts. He did nothing yesterday that had not been practised to perfection like a showbiz routine, and he greeted the cheers and waving of Turkish flags with the gestures of a trouper.

Afterwards, he was as dignified as anyone can be amid the polyglot inanity of an Olympic Press conference. 'It is a pity that my father, mother and brother live in Bulgaria,' he said. 'I haven't seen them. I would like to ask that they be allowed to come to Turkey. There are two million Turkish people in Bulgaria whose names have been changed.' 'One million,' said a voice, presumably Bulgarian. A brief discussion ensued. Eventually, Suleymanoglu's interpreter took over and settled the argument: 'One million, two million, they are people.'

Suleymanoglu also thanked the Bulgarian coach Ivan Abadjiev: 'I will never forget what he did for me.' But at the medals ceremony it was some moments before the champion got round to shaking hands with the vanquished Topourov. When he did he dropped his bouquet (weight about six ounces).

NASTY LITTLE COLD DOES FOR BIG SOVIET LAD
September 1988

Seoul: The troubled weight-lifting competition concluded yesterday, not with the expected super-heavyweight thud but with something very close to a walk-over. The gold medal in the over-110 kg category went to Alexander Kurlovich of the Soviet Union. That may not sound very interesting in itself although, for reasons we shall discuss, it may strike a chord with close students of Canadian police records. But the really interesting part is what happened to the opposition.

The super-heavyweight division was supposed to develop into a great battle between Kurlovich, the Bulgarian Antonio Krastev and the other Soviet lifter, Leonid Taranenko. Krastev, of course, went out of the competition when the Bulgarians slunk home in disgrace having lost two gold medals through positive drug tests. But whatever became of Taranenko?

He was in the hall a few minutes before the competition

began, then was spotted slipping quietly away. The Soviet coach, Alexei Medvedev, said Taranenko had a cold and, because he is 32 years old, the team doctor thought it would be harmful for him to compete. Well, the poor suffering old darling. Taranenko weighs only 22 stone, so he presumably has a very delicate constitution. One is surprised his geriatric nurse even let him travel. Only someone of a vicious turn of mind could consider that there might be an alternative explanation, connected with avoidance of the drugs test. On all known form, Taranenko could have won at least the silver medal as long as he was capable of standing upright. Nasty things, though, colds.

If the super-heavyweight result stands – and every national anthem at these Olympics is played subject to medical ratification – that will leave the Soviet Union with six gold medals and doping control with five victims: the two Bulgarians, two Hungarians on anabolic steroids and a Spaniard who apparently got his prescriptions mixed up. The link between body-building steroids and weight-lifting is well-known, though the Hungarians were so bang to rights that officials were astonished by their lack of sophistication: they would have been caught on the testing equipment used 20 years ago.

The Bulgarians were also a puzzle. They were not caught using steroids, but a diuretic, as recommended by doctors everywhere. Both men moved down a weight category and so had to shed pounds quickly. The explanation could be innocent, except that diuretics also have masking properties and are illegal primarily because they can help cover up steroids. But the Bulgarians knew all that. No nation takes weight-lifting so seriously. They have 22 schools across the country where promising 12-year-olds, for heaven's sake, are sent to be turned into future Olympic champions. How could they make such a stupid mistake?

Everyone was a little bewildered yesterday by that side of the business, though only one person appeared ignorant of the existence of drug-taking. That was the new champion: a nice clean-cut, all-Byelorussian 20-stone boy, from Olga Korbut's home town of Grodno. Asked about steroids

180

yesterday, Kurlovich said: 'What's that?' It was slightly odd that he should ask, since in 1984 he pleaded guilty to smuggling a quantity of them into Canada, was fined a small amount by a Canadian court and banned for life by the Soviet weight-lifting authorities – a sentence reduced to two years after pressure from the international weight-lifting authorities, who thought it too severe.

'We are known as stupid boys in this sport,' said Wolfgang Peter, a member of the International Federation jury, 'so no one is surprised by drugs. You cannot get rid of doping. But we have to fight it.' The fight seems to have been conducted more vigorously in Seoul than at recent world and European championships, and in most categories the amounts lifted have been below records set in other competitions. Kurlovich, for instance, was 10 kg below his own world record and he was well clear of his nearest rivals, two West Germans.

The British team could only look on at all this with a mixture of cynicism and incomprehension. Their super-heavy entrant, Matthew Vine, finished a respectable ninth; and David Morgan came fourth at his weight, 82.5 kg, though this news may have got lost. Morgan did not go to a special weight-lifting school at the age of 12. Indeed, his training for Seoul took place mostly in a small room behind the municipal swimming baths in Cambridge, with the radio for company. He had spent the past year living on dole money and the standard £5,000 grant.

Next week he starts at college in Edinburgh, and he doubts if he will ever be able to try for the Olympics again. 'Can you lend me some money for a hamburger?' he asked his coach, John Lear. 'You must be joking,' said Lear. It is unlikely that Carl Lewis ever has conversations like that. I doubt if Kurlovich ever goes short of a hamburger either.

POOL'S GOLD: A GUILTLESS
SMILE FOR CANADA

October 1988

Seoul: Canada yesterday won its first gold medal of the Games when Carolyn Waldo took the solo event. You may have read something about Canada winning its first gold medal last Saturday in the 100 metres. But one of the peculiarities of the 1988 Olympics is that the figures in the medals table go down as well as up.

This medal, surely, will not be snatched away at dead of night. Synchronised swimming seems to be one of the few guileless, guiltless sports left in the Games. And yet its main function is apparently to be a laughing-stock. This report probably comes over as the upholding of one of the long-standing Olympic traditions: the torch, the flame, and the synchronised swimming mickey-take. Yet the event only arrived in 1984 and has established itself with remarkable speed as one of the Olympics' more telegenic attractions. Maybe it is not sport – what is these days? The purpose of the Olympics should be the pursuit of excellence in whichever field people can express themselves most fluently: be it running, jumping, or water ballet. No one should make fun of synchronised swimming. On the other hand, the temptation is overwhelming.

No one in the crowd had come to mock. The stands had plenty of mums and dads, the sort who must take their holidays at the Korean equivalent of Bridlington and stay up late specially to watch the Asiavision Song Contest.

To other tastes the appeal of the sport is diminished because most of the action takes place under water with only the legs visible, and the participants' features are distorted by their hairpieces and nosepegs. The American competitor, Tracie Ruiz-Conforto, wore a fixed smile reminiscent of a sadistic gym mistress. Britain's girl – Nicola Shearn from Bristol – looked the prettiest. She was not, alas, the best, and her music had evidently been borrowed from a hotel lift. The French girl won musically by a long way: she gave us Holst, Peter Gabriel and Carl Orff.

The real competition came down to a two-girl duel between the North Americans; both managed to use their legs in a way that implied there was a cast of thousands down there. It was most impressive. For the ceremony Tracie let her hair down and started to smile properly. She is really most attractive. She was the champion in 1984, then retired, married a line-backer as all healthy American girls should, and was doing a novelty act with dolphins when her husband persuaded her that she might be better employed having another go at the Olympics.

Carolyn sidestepped the inevitable Ben Johnson question and told the Press she hadn't thought the contest was over until it was over. Tracie agreed: it wasn't over until it was over. The current problem at the Olympics is that events are not over even when they are over, but we will let that pass. During the lengthy translation-pauses between questions Carolyn began to take her hairpiece off, which involved the removal of some 30 pins. This confirmed that the sport requires even more preparation than the average Olympic event.

A few hours later, and a hundred yards away, the rhythmic gymnastics were going on. This is the dry-bob version of synchronised swimming in which girls receive marks for their movement to music with rope, hoop, ribbon and a pair of what are either Indian clubs or chicken drumsticks. The competitors are much younger than those in the pool, smile with less difficulty and show more than the occasional flash of knee. A chap can get into trouble after a day like this. I made an excuse and left.

SWEET SEOUL MUSIC SOOTHES OLYMPICS
October 1988

Seoul: The Olympic Games concluded last night in Seoul in accordance with the script in all important details. The closing ceremony passed off with nothing more alarming than some very loud fireworks.

Juan Antonio Samaranch, the president of the International Olympic Committee, described the Games as 'the best and most universal in our history.' That is true. They were also the most paranoid. Provided Samaranch's luck holds for a few more hours and everyone gets away safely, the thousands of police, soldiers and security men will be stood down with a feeling of relief bordering on amazement. The worst violence of the Olympics came not from North Koreans, terrorists or students but from local boxing officials pummelling a New Zealand referee.

So it was a genuinely happy end to the Olympics. However, these final rites are not to everyone's taste, especially after a hard fortnight. 'Right now,' said one British journalist, 'the only closing ceremony that interests me is last orders in the Dog and Partridge.' But, mercifully, the Olympics shut down a lot quicker and less pompously than they open. Only the flag-bearers had to march on in order. The others appeared behind them as though a sluice-gate had been opened. What followed was a mixture of a tourist promenade round St Mark's Place in high summer, an Aldermaston march, and the final scene of *Sunday Night at the London Palladium* multiplied by 10,000.

There were funny hats, monster masks, New Zealanders carrying signs saying things like 'Hi, Wanganui' and a general end-of-term relaxed silliness. I think it offended the Koreans' sense of order but, as ever, they did their best to smile fixedly through it all. A Canadian athlete carried his baby along papoose-style, which both might have regretted when the fireworks began. Then Steve Cram led a British breakaway group that dashed off and tucked itself in behind the flag-ladies. 'Fastest he's run all effing week,' said someone.

There were a couple of genuinely magical moments. After the three anthems were played – of Greece (who made it all possible), Korea (this year's hosts) and Spain (the next hosts) – the house lights suddenly and dramatically went out. It was either a coup de theatre or a *coup d'état*, and thank heavens it was the first. Then, after the Olympic flag was passed from the Mayor of Seoul to the Mayor of Barcelona, many of the national flag-carriers spontaneously decided to jump on the podium as well. The gesture worked beautifully.

The ritual and the folk dancing went on a little past my attention span, but there were plenty of poignant moments. There was a lantern dance centred on the very spot where Ben Johnson waved to the crowd nine long days ago. And there was a time, when the cymbals were crashing and the searchlights dancing, when one wondered if all this might be carrying 40 miles away where North Korean soldiers stare unblinkingly and uncomprehendingly at the outside world across the DMZ.

The 1988 Olympics have been a political triumph for the host country in a way unmatched since the Tokyo Games of 1964. The full implications of that should unfold in the months ahead. In a few weeks South Korea may once more revert to being the Land of the Morning Calm. But it is unlikely to be regarded ever again as the Hermit Kingdom.

The main crisis the Olympic movement faces now is over drugs, which is not something for which anyone can blame the Koreans. In other respects, the IOC can look ahead to the next Games with an optimism that it had almost forgotten. There will doubtless be some ghastliness between now and 1992 to change all that. But for the moment, for the first time, it is possible to imagine an Olympics in which every country on earth is represented, barring South Africa. And even there, perhaps, the future cannot be delayed forever.

The majority of the most vivid images of the 1988 Olympics will be those that represent the triumph of the human spirit – Ngugi's amazing run in the 5,000 metres; Louganis bashing his head on the springboard and carrying on regardless; the weight-lifter Suleymanoglu defeating politics and gravity ...

For the journalist here the television images are always less memorable than reality: the 4 a.m. phone call giving the news of Johnson's dope test; the long hotel lobby watches waiting for the Medical Commission to pronounce; the morning scramble for the bus; kidney beans again in the Press canteen. But it could all have been very much worse and in the past it has been.

When American television wound up its coverage, the first post-Olympic ad on Seoul's US army station was a public service message about drugs: Just say no. That may yet have to become the Olympic motto, and fast. There are just 1,400 steroid-taking days before Barcelona.

OAKLAND FAIL OREL EXAM
October 1988

Oakland, California: To the astonishment of a nation, the new champions of baseball are the Los Angeles Dodgers, who won the World Series early yesterday, beating the Oakland Athletics by four games to one. The Dodgers took the last game in Oakland 5-2 rendering the last two contests of the series unnecessary. Since the travelling fan is an almost unknown beast in the United States, the climax of the season came amid something as close to silence as you can get in a stadium with 50,000 people present. Part of the silence was due to bewilderment.

The Athletics had surged imperiously through the long, hot summer and the play-offs. The Dodgers arrived almost apologetically with a batting line-up that looked outclassed before the series began and was then so wracked by injury they could hardly field a team. 'They're so good compared to us, they should allow us two runs before the start,' said Tommy Lasorda, the Los Angeles manager.

That proved unnecessary. Lasorda's No 1 pitcher, Orel Hershiser IV, delivered the goods spectacularly in the fifth game, as he had done before. The opposition's two overpowering sluggers, Jose Canseco and Mike McGwire – christened the Bash Brothers by the Oakland marketing department – had only one hit each in 36 attempts between them. After 42 and 32 home runs respectively during the regular season, it was just about their only unproductive week all year.

To what extent Lasorda's special blend of Italian-American blarney was also a factor remains mysterious. He is a sort of one-man roadshow and sometimes gets written off as a clown.

However, he swears by his players, and vice-versa. 'I'll tell you,' he said. 'If there are people who doubt themselves, who feel they can't make it in life, they should look at this ball club and let it be an inspiration to them. Anyone can do it if they want to do it badly enough.' Lasorda has managed the Dodgers for 12 years in a business where managers come and go like temps. He has a unique mixture of proven managerial competence, folksiness and ethnic appeal. He should be running for President, dammit.

His team seemed to be held together with sticking plaster. The vital runs last night all came from players discarded by other teams: Mike Davis, who was a failure with Oakland, and Mickey Hatcher and Rick Dempsey, who were drifting out of the sport and then rang the Dodgers to ask if there was a vacancy for them. This does not happen in real life.

The Dodgers, however, have always had a reputation as a shrewdly run club and this is a triumph for their entire well-oiled organisation – and for one pitcher in particular: Orel Hershisher was named Most Valuable Player of the Series and is now being compared to the great pitchers of history. Part of that comes from natural talent: a lot of it is hard work. His rich father (Orel III) hired a major league player to coach him when he was a boy, and Orel IV uses a personal computer to file information about the opposition. He was asked what sort of computer it was, but declined to answer: 'The advertising deal hasn't been signed yet.'

In non-financial matters Hershiser is almost unworldly. He kept calm in the last game by singing hymns to himself and then thanked the Lord for his success before mentioning the mortals who have helped him. He is a very serious young man and one was inclined to think that he might be the only baseball player in California who thinks coke is a drink. But several other Dodgers made religious allusions after the game. It seems the tradition of big, bad, roistering baseball players that dates back to Babe Ruth and beyond is in decline.

One thing that does not change is the crowd reaction. Until the moment of defeat the atmosphere in Oakland was marvellous, with that loudmouthed but utterly unthreatening innocence that pervades American sporting gatherings. This was nothing like a soccer crowd – the chanters, whoopers, yellers and rooters were probably all in highly paid computer jobs – and nothing like a cricket crowd either.

It is strange and chastening for anyone steeped in our summer game to see all this. I will always love cricket and can only fancy this as a bit on the side. But baseball is a great game because the less ignorant you become, the more engrossing it is. That is even truer for cricket. It is not true for one-day cricket, which gets tedious with repetition. Traditional cricket is a more aesthetic and complex game than baseball and as such the more satisfying in the end. But cricket has much to learn, and envy. Baseball crowds were the highest ever in 1988 for the fourth year running. The sport has successfully adapted to the commercial pressures of the age, yet remained in essence true to itself.

Contrast that with cricket: torn apart by global politics and maladministration – and now facing growing apathy in most Test-playing countries towards the time-honoured form of the game. Baseball knows what it is and where it is going; cricket has not got a clue. This is not to suggest that Lord's immediately ought to start playing rock music over the loudspeakers between innings or hire someone to wander around the Warner Stand dressed as a chicken. But baseball has achieved great things through high class leadership: the Oakland club, for instance, is owned by the Haas family who own Levi Strauss. They know a thing or two about marketing. Cricket desperately needs a fraction of that expertise to replace all the complacency and pig ignorant snobbery.

ON THE SUNNY SIDE OF THE STREET
March 1989

After England's last soccer international BBC's *Sportsnight* did a feature on the tabloid football press, showing the reporters phoning their London offices from Athens, receiving advice on how to report the game they had just seen and instructions on exactly how to inject the curare into the manager's anatomy. One viewer watched with more-than-normal horror because he knows a thing or two about popular sports journalism, or at least he thought he did.

His name is Desmond Hackett, which may not mean a lot now. But in his day, which stretched from the 1930s to the 1970s, Hackett really was somebody: the original legend in his own lunchtime, the sports reporter as superstar. Even now *Private Eye* occasionally pays him a tribute by by-lining its soccer cod-pieces 'Desmond Hack.'

He worked for the *Daily Express* when it was a bigger newspaper than it is these days in every sense of the word – when Beaverbrook held sway, the circulation nudged five million, and Brian Inglis wrote that a Fleet Street journalist who had not worked for the *Express* was like a soldier who had never marched towards the sound of gunfire. The leading paper these days is the *Sun* and its soldiers rely on poison gas and fragmentation bombs.

If England lose to Albania tomorrow – and quite likely even if they win – the tabloids will again attack Bobby Robson, though, when you have already used headlines such as 'In the Name of God, Go', it must be difficult to know what to say to show you are really angry. Hackett savoured that headline for a minute: 'Stupid, isn't it? It's still a bloody game.'

He is 76 now, unsteady on his pins but otherwise thriving in his flat near Clapham South station. Since he retired from the *Express*, early and with some acrimony, he has not written a word. This week, he will admit, he feels a pang: Albania is the only country in Europe he never visited.

Ah, but the places he did go, and the things he did: he trained Don Cockell, turned up at Muhammad Ali's hospital bedside before an operation wearing a white coat ('Don't worry,' he said when the champ recognised him. 'I'm only going to watch.') and he scooped the world on the four-minute mile.

He danced with Vivien Leigh, kissed Mary Pickford ('Beat that, mate.'), made a record with Eddie Fisher, taught Tito's wife how to twist, had tea poured all over him by Peron, challenged Chou-en-Lai to a game of table tennis, and I bet at least half these stories are true.

You cannot, however, be quite sure. The point about Hackett's journalism is that it was not based on a slavish regard for facts. 'You'd get an idea,' he says, 'and you'd draw the truth towards it.' Roy Ullyett, an old chum and the *Express* cartoonist, put it another way: 'Vaudeville in print, it was. The idea was to get people talking.'

At that Hackett never failed. He was not a great man of letters or even a real expert on the sports he covered. But he was sharp-eyed, quick witted, bombastic and inventive. He once described the golfer Bobby Locke walking away 'with the affronted air of an archbishop slapped on the back and called 'Arry Boy.' He sold newspapers.

The Hackett trademark was his brown bowler hat. Once he promised to kick it down Fleet Street if Arsenal won a European game. In 1967 he offered to walk barefoot home from Wembley if Chelsea won the Cup. That was after the third round; they reached the final (losing to Spurs) and the *Express* had a gimmick for months. Thousands of stickers appeared saying 'Get walking, Hackett.' Another time he promised to clean Jack Bodell's windows if he won a fight. If Hackett was right, fine; if he was wrong, so much the better.

He was the most famous representative of an old journalistic school which believed in great truths, such as sportsmanship and the amateur principle, and did not worry too much about small ones. Some of his colleagues still marvel at Hackett's epic account of how he had his shirt ripped from his back during the 'Battle of Berne' in the 1954 World Cup and wonder most of all how it occurred without him ever leaving the press box.

Hackett smiles a little sheepishly when these sort of stories are mentioned. 'Well, if you see it happen, it detracts from the story. I have never looked back and said I hurt anyone's feelings. It's my main claim to fame.'

Because he was influential and charming, people would go along with his, shall we say, factional approach to sports reporting. Soccer clubs and boxing managers would co-operate in bogus injury scares and then knock them down next day. He wrote cheerfully for a paper that liked it that way and lived accordingly: 'Dear old Des,' said Ullyett. 'You felt alive when you were with him, even if you felt half dead the next morning.'

Somewhere along the way this carefree form of journalism mutated into the twilight world of the modern tabloid sports pages. The money that used to be spent on Hackett's unlimited expenses now, on several papers, goes on cheques to footballers with a grudge and an agent. 'It's a nasty business,' said Hackett. 'When I say business, I mean business. When I say nasty, I mean nasty. It's very seldom you see a sporting gesture either on the field or in print.'

So what changed? Sports journalists are inclined to say that television finished him. People could see games for themselves and his engagingly fanciful stuff became outdated. Ullyett thinks people began taking themselves and their sport too seriously. Hackett blames sport's obsession with money. He insists he never paid a penny for a footballer's exclusive; no one thought that way. 'I went up to Preston one day to take Tom Finney an offer to sign for Juventus – £50,000 for signing on, an enormous wage, a villa and a car, you know, the real stuff. He said: "It sounds all right, Desmond. But I don't think the club would like it." '

I don't entirely swallow Hackett's rosy view of the past. But, as he says, football is supposed to be a game and if England do lose to Albania it would be nice to believe that journalists will see it in reasonable perspective. Hackett would have done, whatever liberties he might have taken with the details. Some of his successors act like Ayatollahs, with Robson playing the part of Rushdie.

'ERE WE GO, 'ERE WE GO WITH THE FIGHTING DUTCHMEN
March 1989

Eindhoven: So I asked this policeman on Amsterdam central station where to buy a ticket for the football train. He said: 'Are you sure?' I nodded without conviction. He shrugged, led me round the corner and pointed to the far side of the concourse where the city's youth were staging a re-enactment of feeding time at a medieval asylum. 'Good luck,' he said.

That was on Sunday, hours before the biggest match of the Dutch domestic soccer season: PSV Eindhoven, the leading club in the country, at home to the most famous, Ajax Amsterdam. Yesterday Eindhoven's main drinking street, the Stratumseind, was still covered in broken glass and general debris; 30 people had been arrested, and two taken to hospital. Routine, said the police.

It has always been hard to take the stories about soccer hooliganism in Holland all that seriously. Since the 17th century we have regarded the Dutch as nice, progressive people who are particularly good with houseplants. One look at Amsterdam station said the truth was horrid.

The four ticket windows dealing with football fans were only open for half an hour; the hordes shoved and seethed while sensible burghers, queuing nearby for tickets, to their tulipy suburbs, looked on amazed. By the time the relieved clerks pulled down the blinds marked 'Gesloten' three of the four windows had been smashed. Someone celebrated by letting off a firecracker. You might as well start the day as you mean to go on.

Dutch football yobbery is a late-Eighties phenomenon which has started to pose a serious threat to a tolerant and libertarian nation. This game may have been the last major occasion before the Government imposes a limited ID-card scheme which will apply to travelling supporters of the five worst-affected clubs, including Ajax and PSV.

There are similarities to the English experience, and differences. Both are fascinating. One major difference is that the opposition to the cards is being co-ordinated by supporters' tribunes who emerged from the terraces. They met in Utrecht on Saturday and, with lawyers, agreed on a plan to challenge the law on constitutional grounds. Then the Ajax fans told the PSV people: 'We'll kill you tomorrow.' Some of the head-bangers on 'F-side', the Ajax kop, would not treat that as a figure of speech.

Before being allowed on the train, they were searched for

alcohol and weapons. This being Holland, they were allowed to keep their marijuana, which was no bad thing. Many lads spent the 90-minute journey looking distinctly mellow and throughout the train there was a sweet smell.

All the kids were, almost without exception, longer haired and more stylishly dressed than their British counterparts. One looked around nervously for signs of the toytown Nazism that has become the motif of English hooligans.

But Ajax are known throughout Holland as 'the Jews' because, like Tottenham, the club was traditionally Jewish-run. The fans have decided to take this as a compliment and F-side has adopted the Israeli flag as its symbol. Many of the fans wore Star of David earrings. By the time the train reached Eindhoven, the star had been marked on strategic walls all over the carriages.

As well as this addition, there were some subtractions. Some of the youths were distinctly unmellow. As we passed through one football town, Utrecht, only toilet rolls went through the window; but at another, Den Bosch, there were light fittings. Several seats were smashed up. The handful of police, who could not have done much about it without shooting everybody, remained passive.

When we arrived, F-side trotted towards the stadium with the air of an overwhelmingly superior army going over the top. 'What do you think of PSV?' I asked one, rather bright youth. 'They are cowards, they run away.' 'The supporters or the team?' 'Of course, the supporters. The players all come from Ajax, anyway.' 'Will there be fighting?' I asked another. 'I hope so,' he said.

I was evolving the theory that this was a universal rite of early manhood. After all, Italian fans had to be caged in 20 years ago when English football grounds were quieter than the universities. But at the stadium it became obvious where the Dutch had learnt all this.

Their chants, in almost every case, were stolen wholesale. They have fitted Dutch words to 'Hark the Herald Angels Sing' but everything else was imported without translation. 'Wem-ber-ley ... Wem-ber-ley ...', ''ere we go ...' 'You'll Never Walk Alone.' The lot. Holland is always the most

193

eclectic of countries, picking up ideas from all around. But this borders on British cultural imperialism: they gave us a lager; we gave them loutishness.

On the field, it was a great day for Ajax. PSV started six points clear of them at the top of the table, and had not lost at home in five years; victory would have almost settled the championship. Instead, Ajax won 4-1 and for the first hour, until they went 3-0 up and the tension subsided, it was an absolutely brilliant match, everything one could expect of the best two teams in the champion European footballing nation.

Eindhoven supporters took defeat very quietly. The club is owned by the Philips company, like most of the district; the team won the European Cup last year and the stadium is magnificent. But the people are bumpkins compared to Amsterdammers and for the most part allowed themselves to be taunted, merely throwing the occasional lump of concrete into the argument. Ajax supporters greeted their team's arrival with flares, and each time they scored rattled the bars of their cage enough to terrify the police dogs.

I caught only one flash of humour: when the Ajax fans sang 'Y viva España' to mark PSV's European Cup defeat last week against Real Madrid. Dutch football has not yet caught up with the new jokey post-brutalism of English soccer. Perhaps next year F-side will start carrying inflatable rabbis.

The supporters have, however, started to use their political strength. The ID cards already exist but so far have only been used for little perks and concessions, not as a condition for admission. The F-side regulars have resolutely refused to buy them.

A big test of will comes next month. Holland are playing West Germany, a game that involves deadly serious national passions. The Dutch FA are only selling tickets to card holders.

The Dutch scheme is not supposed to be used as a general national sledgehammer, and this ploy seems designed to tempt F-side and their allies into submission. I suppose if the yobs respond by boycotting matches, that is hardly a disaster; but if they turn to violence elsewhere, it might be.

Meanwhile, back in Stratumseind, municipal workers were

194

yesterday clearing up the mess. Next week Den Haag, currently in the second division but still with a reputation for having the nastiest supporters of all, are in town for a match against another Eindhoven club. 'Luckily,' said one bar keeper, 'I only have small windows.'

THE GRIEF OF SOCCER'S KENNEDY CLAN
April 1989

Anfield Road is much less grand than you might think, hardly more than a side street edged by Victorian villas. But opposite are the Bill Shankly Memorial Gates, above them the words 'You'll Never Walk Alone' and next to them the walls topped with the spikes, razor wire and broken glass that signify a modern football ground.

People began arriving there yesterday soon after dawn and by mid-morning there was an almost constant stream of mourners. They queued at the florist's stall outside the cemetery on the other side of Stanley Park, then cut through to place their flowers by the gates, and sometimes their scarves and bobble hats, too.

At lunchtime the directors decided to let the public in. The flowers were placed in the goal net at the Kop end, on the barriers behind and, as more people arrived with their tributes, along the Kop itself. Perhaps 1,000 people stood by the goal close to the 'Do not go on the pitch' sign. There was no sound except muffled sobbing. Some moved on quickly; others stayed, staring numbly. A tough-looking man in a leather jacket stood crying, probably for the first time in years; an old man in a shabby coat waited close by for at least two hours, moving only to help two lads tie their hats to the railings and to take the occasional slug of whisky. Four little girls in Sunday dresses came along with single tulips. But the more elaborate bunches had messages: 'Everton FC Supporters. Our condolences. We pray for the lads who loved Liverpool FC'; 'Look after them, Shanks, from all the lads at Kirkby'; and again and again and again: 'You'll never walk alone.'

No other football club has such a beautiful phrase so closely associated with it. And at no other club would the aftermath of a chance disaster to spectators focus so strongly on the club and not the dead and bereaved themselves. Liverpool have become the Kennedy family of sport, for whom great triumphs and great emotion have been sundered by great tragedies. But in Anfield, the district rather than the football ground, life was going on. Along with the mourners in Anfield Road there were men walking dogs and children on bicycles.

Soon it was possible to hear the whistling and shouting of football matches coming from Stanley Park, 300 yards away, from where it is possible to see both the Liverpool and Everton grounds. The committee of the Anfield Junior Soccer League had met on Saturday night and decided there should be a minute's silence then the semi-finals of the under-11s League cup should go ahead. 'My lad was at Hillsborough,' Ronnie Fawcett, one of the team managers, said. 'It was three hours before I found out he'd only hurt his leg. Someone was screaming at him for help but he was just carried forward on the surge and couldn't do anything. We both feel drained. But you've got to go on, otherwise when do you start? We shall all feel the same next Sunday.'

So far as anyone knew, none of the under-11s due to play had been to Sheffield and not come back. But no one was certain. The city was subsisting on rumour and everyone knew someone who knew someone of whom they had heard nothing.

Just down the road at St Columba's, the local Roman Catholic church, a young preacher told his congregation that the suffering would not last for ever. 'Because Jesus rose from the dead, we know death is not the end.' Only two months ago the Anglican Bishop of Liverpool evoked that image on another football matter: the identity-card debate in the House of Lords. 'Many people have little sense of belonging or counting or identity,' he said. 'I don't want to exaggerate, but following a football team gives you many of these experiences, something to be proud of, success that is yours to share in. Indeed, sometimes laps of honour, bringing the Cup home, have the feel of the liturgy of the Resurrection.'

But the liturgy of football is usually altogether different. On the bridges along the M62 there are slogans placed by Liverpool's supporters to taunt Manchester United's fans: 'Munich '58.' Football slogans and songs have become the basest currency but perhaps Liverpool now has it right: 'Walk on, walk on, with hope in your heart.' When the grieving ends, that is all anyone can do.

A FINAL TO FORGET
May 1989

As a small group of us wandered through the bowels of Wembley after the game, a man in a Liverpool scarf came up and asked if we were journalists. We nodded, cagily. 'We've won the Cup,' he said, 'and I don't care.

'I've spent about 40 hours since Hillsborough writing to the papers defending Liverpool fans. I won't do it again, I'm disgusted. I know there was no violence. It was just disrespect. The administrators for once treated the fans like human beings and they've responded by shitting on them.'

What can one say? In the last 40 minutes of Saturday's final there were seven pitch invasions – one for each of the four late goals, one when the crowd thought the game was over, another when it really was – and before all that a lone Evertonian nutter ran on and abused Trevor Steven. Perhaps we should just blame him; all the trouble was essentially imitative and each time the average age of the invaders grew younger.

On the face of it, this was not a very bad day by footballing standards. But, as good days go, it was dreadfully depressing. Hillsborough was only five weeks ago. Just two weeks ago Liverpool won a semi-final at Old Trafford on a day when the numbness wore off to be replaced by an emotional bond linking the players and every spectator. That bond is not just fraying already, but snapping. Oh, yes, it was all good-humoured and safe: if Liverpool and Everton fans habitually attacked each other, everyday life in the city would have ceased long ago, and, of course, only a small minority ran on. But as the crowd strutted up from the tube station, clutching The Great British Breakfast – a four-pack of lager – one sensed that football was getting back to its old self.

If a game like this at a time like this is so close to the edge, then the future is very bleak. The fences at Wembley were going back up anyway; now they will never come down. The idea that major football matches can be played without some form of pitch protection bit the dust on Saturday; and the concept of light-touch policing, the opposite of the South Yorkshire approach, received a severe setback.

Perhaps people were expecting too much of the occasion. Even the preliminaries failed to work. Gerry the Pacemaker's version of You'll Never Walk Alone is rather longer than the Anfield rendition, and the terraces were way ahead of him: they sang it better when they were supposed to be singing the National Anthem. Gerry then attempted to lead the crowd in Abide With Me, but neither he nor they knew the words, and when he faltered there was nothing.

The old magic of the Cup final community singing, traditionally led by a dignified gent named Arthur Caiger, disappeared 20 years ago when the ground was fully enclosed and the words stopped rolling magnificently round the stadium. That probably also marks the time when football fans ceased to be imbued with Sunday-school ethics and education. The one minute's silence held – just about.

There are days when I feel old and crabby and this was one of them: I found it hard to accept as a classic a match in which nothing happened between the fourth and 89th minutes. But it was a good day for football's Governmental enemies, not just because it may have improved the political prospects of the Minister for Sport's benighted bill, but because it reinforced the traditionally pessimistic Hobbesian Tory view of basic human nature.

A FALLEN OLYMPIAN COMES CLEAN
June 1989

Toronto: Ben Johnson's stint in the witness box in Toronto lasted barely seven hours, far less than expected. He wasted little time on polysyllables or coherent sentences, and the lawyers were notably gentle with him.

After they had finished, the Commissioner, Mr Justice Dubin, said he would like a word. He was clutching a copy of the interview Johnson gave on his return in disgrace from Seoul last year, in which the sprinter proclaimed his innocence, saying that someone had switched the samples, and demanded an inquiry.

'I think,' said the judge, 'it's fair to say most Canadians wanted to believe that. You understand that – everybody felt kindly towards you?'

'Yes.'

'Did you not realise how important it was – what a disservice it was to sign a statement like that?'

'I did wrong. But, like I say, I was confused at the time.'

'Your lawyer has said you got a lot of letters of support from young people.'

Johnson rose to the bait. 'Thousands of letters, yes,' he said proudly.

'Who all believed you were innocent, right?'

'Yes,' said Johnson, much more quietly.

The inquiry has so far used up 58 days, 63 witnesses, 10,000 pages of transcripts and millions of dollars.

Innocence is a relative matter. We know now, if anyone had not already guessed it, that Johnson took drugs and then lied. Whether he is a dupe with the IQ of a nine-year-old or a shrewder cookie than he lets on remains a matter of dispute. But it is generally agreed that, as one of his team-mates put it, he is no rocket scientist.

The real innocent here is the mild-mannered and earnest nation which set up the inquiry. Visiting journalists regularly make fun of Canada. There is something about these grey countries, such as Belgium and New Zealand, in which people lead well-fed, contented, private and apolitical lives, which is fundamentally bad for business. Why can't they be interesting, dammit, like China or Iran?

In sport, the Canadians have tried hard to be interesting. In 1976, at the Montreal Olympics, Canada emerged, humiliated, from its own show without a single gold medal. Then it began to work on serious, subsidised sports programmes. Only two years later, at the Edmonton Commonwealth Games, Canada finished top of the medals table. The Sports Minister announced, triumphantly, 'We won the Games' – a concept no one else had considered before, still less crowed about. By the 1980s they had a genuine star to crow about: Ben Johnson.

In mid-scandal there was a half-hearted attempt to disown him ('Canada wins gold; Jamaican immigrant loses it'), but Canadians, like everyone else, want to believe the best of Ben. Already there is talk of forgiveness once his mandatory two-year ban ends next year. Dick Pound, the Canadian vice-president of the IOC, has pointed out that a two-year ban to an athlete is like a 20-year sentence to a criminal. People are even beginning to look forward to his comeback.

The inquiry is very Canadian. Can you imagine the British Government spending money to discover something as trivial as the truth? Canada, still puzzled and hurt, has acted as though steroids were its own problem and it has done everyone a great service. The long, boring days in the anonymous Toronto office block may help cleanse the world.

Johnson is a liar, but his wheedling coach told him something close to the truth: 'The whole world is using drugs.' Of course, there are clean sportsmen. But, while Johnson has been humiliated, there are countless others who have not been caught; big names, honoured names, British names.

On the wall of the inquiry press room there is a list of 54 drugs to help us with our spelling. They range from aqueous testosterone to yohimbine; pink pills, blue pills; milky-white stuff, reddish-brown liquid; taken in the mouth, taken up the bum. The list is by no means exhaustive.

The phenomenon Johnson noticed, breast enlargement, is known to members of the subculture as 'bitch tits', a well-known side-effect. There is another called 'steroid rage' – depression and aggression. No one can know the consequences of all these drugs; the long-term implications to the liver, the heart, the sexual organs and the brain.

The dangers may be greatest to athletes not in organised drug rings like Johnson's, but those training alone in sports and countries where lavish funding is not available, people who might be desperate enough to exceed the stated dose. Countries like Britain, actually.

Success in many sports now involves a Faustian deal with anabolic steroids. And there is increasing evidence that it is spreading beyond the successful – between six and 11 per cent of 16 and 17-year-olds in American high schools, according to recent surveys – and even beyond sportsmen to kids convinced that building up their muscles will help them pull girls. This is a more than normally bad idea if one of the consequences is impotence.

We are not talking about casual, recreational drug use or an attempt to re-create the hysterical inanity that surrounded Ian Botham's use of marijuana. We are talking about children, and those little older than that, feeling compelled to alter their bodies chemically to compete, whether in sport or socially.

If Johnson's fall helps alert everyone to the problem, he will deserve more than reinstatement: he should get a knighthood.